PARENT-TEEN MANUAL FOR LEARNING TO DRIVE

A STEP BY STEP GUIDE
FOR LEARNING HOW TO DRIVE
SAFELY AND EFFICIENTLY

WARREN P. QUENSEL
Former Teacher and
State Supervisor

SAFETY ENTERPRISES
Bloomington, Illinois

These lessons are based on two decades of teaching experiences and driver task analysis studies. Grateful acknowledgment is made to the many colleagues for their suggestions and field testing of the original materials.

ISBN 0-9636134-0-5

Printed in the United States of America
SAFETY ENTERPRISES
1010 South Summit
Bloomington, Illiinos
309/828-0906

CONTENTS

HOW TO USE THE MANUAL

This Manual was developed for students, instructors, and especially parents. This is because teenagers must receive much additional supervised practice driving experiences if they are to become safe drivers. By providing about fifty hours of supervised practice in the family car, parents can help make a real reduction in the teenage collision rates. The parent supervising such practice will be identified as "Coach" in the Manual.

The Coach and student should read the complete Manual for a brief overview of the lessons. Then, the student should study each lesson and memorize the main points before coming to practice. Those students enrolled in a school program should complete at least the first three lessons before practicing in the family car.

At the end of each lesson, there are activities and coaching tips for the parent to follow. Here are some general guidelines to follow for all lessons.

1. The family car to be used should have an outside mirror on the right side. A mirror attached to the sun visor could be helpful.

2. A good system of communication should be agreed on at the outset so each person knows what to expect of the other. Plan turns one block ahead. When giving directions, always tell where first. Then tell what action is to be taken.

3. The Coach should make an analysis of the various areas of the community. Beginners should not be put into situations they are not ready for. If a dangerous situation comes up, pull over and wait.

4. The Coach should learn to "read" the traffic scene around the car, and at the same time observe the feet and hands of the driver. If a long explanation is needed, stop in a safe place for a discussion.

5. The Coach's posture should be one of relaxed alertness. The left hand needs to be in a position for immediate access to the lower half of the steering wheel. In case of an emergency, the selector lever can be put in neutral, and if need be, the engine could be shut off. Be calm and patient but alert.

LESSON 1
STARTING AND STOPPING HABITS

In the first lesson, students will learn the proper use of the controls for starting the engine, moving the car forward and backward, and stopping. These habits are basic to all other driving skills and should last a lifetime. The proper use of controls can save fuel and pollution.

The car controls differ from car to car, and each has its own set of "feels". They are easy to use, but their proper use will take practice. Beginners need time to learn what to expect from the improper or rough use of the controls as well as their smooth and well coordinated use.

PRE-DRIVING CHECKS

As you walk to the car, get into the habit of looking around and under the car. Under the hood checks can be made while you are stopped for gasoline.

Outside the Car Checks

1. Check the body for dents and clear air vents.

2. Check for toys and other objects nearby.

3. Check the direction of the front wheels.

4. Check the tires for uneven wear and inflation.

    ..Properly inflated tires give better gas mileage.

    ..Check the air pressure once a month when the tires are cold.

5. Check the pavement for liquid leaks.

    ..Yellowish-green is from the radiator or hoses.

    ..Reddish color is from the transmission or the power steering.

    ..Black or dark brown is oil from the engine.

    ..Clear water is from the air conditioner.

Under the Hood Checks

1. Check the radiator fluid level.

2. Check the windshield washer fluid level.

3. Check the dip stick for oil level.

4. Check the battery cables for corrosion.

5. Check the drive belts for looseness and cracks.

Inside the Car Checks and Adjustments

1. Place key in the ignition and lock the doors.

   ..Provides better protection during a crash.

   ..Prevents strangers entering at traffic stops.

2. Check for objects on shelf under rear window.

3. Adjust seat and head restraints.

4. Adjust mirrors and sun visor.

5. Adjust the lap and shoulder belts. (See owner's manual)

6. Identify and operate the light switches.

7. Identify and operate the windshield wipers.

8. Identify and operate the air conditioner or heater switches and controls.

STARTING THE ENGINE

Check the owner's manual for the proper steps to follow when starting a cold engine, a warm engine, and a flooded engine. The fumes from the exhaust contain a poisoness gas. So, do not start or run the engine in a closed garage.

Check the Selector Lever and Park Brake

The park brake will prevent the car from rolling if an error is made. It is best to start the engine in P(park) unless the car stalls in traffic. Then N(neutral) is best. On older cars there may be a need to set the automatic choke.

Turn Key to ON and Check the Gauges

After turning the key to ON, hesitate briefly to see that the warning lights and gauges are working. Light bulbs do burn out.

On is the normal engine running position.

Start switches on the starter motor which turns over the engine.

Off allows the engine to be turned off without locking the steering wheel and the selector lever. This position can be used for pushing or towing the car.

Acc permits the operation of the radio and other accessories when the engine is not running.

Lock is the only position for removing the key. The steering wheel and ignition are locked to prevent theft.

Turn the Key to Start and Release

As the sound of the engine is heard, release the key and it will return to the **On** position. The starter motor should not be operated for more than a few seconds at a time. Holding the key to **Start** while the engine is running will cause a whirring sound and chipped gears.

Read Gauges as the Engine Slows to Normal Idle

A cold engine will start at a fast idle before slowing to a normal idle. If the engine vibrates or misses while idling, it may be a sign that adjustments need to be made by mechanic. As the engine idles, make sure the battery is charging and the oil pressure is okay. When you allow the engine to warm up for more than one minute, gasoline is wasted. The best way to warm up a cold engine and car is to drive slowly a few blocks.

Adjust the Air Vents and Defroster

Air vents bring outside air into the car. Make sure the air inlets in front of the windshield are not covered with leaves or snow. The defroster clears the windshield of ice on the outside and fogging over on the inside.

MOVING THE CAR FORWARD

Hold the Foot Brake Down

Pushing the foot brake down prevents the car from moving and can avoid costly repairs.

Place the Selector Lever in "D"

`P  R N D 2 1`

Drive (D) is used for all normal driving conditions. Check the owner's manual for the proper use of "2" and "1". If the car has a tendency to lurch forward, the engine may be idling too fast.

Release the Brakes

It is best to keep the park brake on until the car is to be moved. After the park brake is off, release the foot brake.

Press Gently on the Gas Pedal

Form the habit of pressing on the gas pedal gently. Imagine there is an egg between your foot and the pedal. Learn how much pressure to use by noting the sounds and "feels" of the car.

As the car increases speed, the transmission will automatically shift gears. You should be able to feel the shifting at speeds of about 12 mph and 18 mph. The car will shift more smoothly if you ease up slightly on the pressure at these speeds. This saves gasoline and wear on the transmission.

Remember

Brake down - Lever to D - Brake up - Gas down

STOPPING THE CAR

Release the Gas Pedal

A car starts slowing down as soon as the gas pedal is released except on a downhill. Releasing the gas pedal before braking saves gasoline and wear on the foot brakes.

Press Brake Pedal to Point of Resistance

For a smooth stop, begin well before the stopping point. Push the brake pedal down gradually, and use a firm but steady pressure. If you are not slowing fast enough, push a little more. If you are stopping too soon, ease up a little.

4

Apply Full Pressure

To come to a complete stop, apply and maintain full pressure on the brake pedal. If the brakes are applied quickly and too hard, there will be a weight transfer from the rear end to the front end. This causes the front end to nose down which affects steering and braking control.

Types of Braking Actions

Cover Brake -- This involves placing your foot over the brake pedal without putting pressure on the brakes. Reaction time is reduced.

Light Braking -- This is a steady and light pressure on the brake pedal for a gradual slowing down.

Medium or Normal Braking -- This involves a gradual pressure on the brake pedal until the car stops.

Hard Braking -- For an emergency, this involves a hard, quick push on the brakes all the way down. If the pedal is held down, the wheels will lock and the tires will slide to a stop. Then, steering control will be lost.

To keep steering control in an emergency, "squeeze" the brake pedal hard until the wheels just about lock-up. Then, release the pedal pressure slightly and "squeeze" the pedal again. Many new cars are now equipped with an anti-lock braking system (ABS) which allows the car to be steered during hard braking. Expect some vibration of the brake pedal when this system is used. Never pump the brakes on a car so equipped.

SECURING THE CAR FOR PARKING

Never leave your car unattended with the engine running. Develop a habit of following certain steps when securing the car. This helps prevent forgetting any steps which could lead to theft or the car rolling away.

Place the Selector Lever in Park

The **P** position will lock the transmission and hold the car in place. Be sure the car has completely stopped moving before placing the selector lever in park. Otherwise, serious damage can result.

Shut Off All Accessories

Turn off the radio, heater fan, air conditioner, and any other electrical devices. This prevents an undue drain on the battery when starting the engine.

Turn Key to Lock and Set the Park Brake

Shut off the engine by turning the key to lock so you can remove the key. To provide extra protection against the car rolling away, set the parking brake.

Remove the Restraints and Lock the Doors

Remove the safety belts carefully so they don't get out of adjustment or caught in the door. It is wise to open the door with your right hand so you will have to look back to check traffic. Hold the keys in your left hand until the door is closed.

MOVING THE CAR BACKWARD

Brake and Shift to R   P R N D 2 1

Make sure your car is not moving before shifting to reverse. Otherwise, the transmission could be damaged. Hold the brake down until you are ready to move.

Look Toward the Intended Path

It is important to get into a position to see along the car's intended path. Twist your body around to the right for a view to the rear. Use your right hand to help brace yourself. Make quick glances to the front and sides to be sure your car is not getting off the intended path.

Keep One Hand at the Top of Steering Wheel

The back of your car will go in the direction the top of the steering wheel is turned. You should need only slight steering actions to back along a straight path.

Release the Brake and Creep

Creep backwards by releasing the brake. Control the speed by moving your foot back and forth between the brake and gas pedal. Take your time and back slowly.

ACTIVITIES' AND COACHING TIPS

1. While the family car is parked in a garage or driveway, have student follow the car owner's manual to make under the hood checks.

2. The Coach should drive the family car to an off-street area, such as a parking lot. If such an area is not available, a straight stretch of a level street (500 feet) should be selected in a quiet residential area.

3. As the car is driven to the practice area, the Coach should explain the use of controls, switches, and gauges. At the practice area, the student is asked to explain outside and inside car checks and adjustments. Be sure student can locate all controls. A cushion should be available for short students.

4. Have the student use all the controls first before starting the engine. Then, the engine is started and shut off several times before the car is moved. Read the gauges aloud and explain what they mean.

5. The new driver should then be drilled on moving the car forward a few feet, stopping, and turning the engine off. Repeat four or five times. Make sure the steps are repeated in correct order until they can be performed without hesitation. Give student a chance to make hard and medium braking actions.

6. Have the student move the car back a few feet and stop. Repeat until the car is back to the starting point. The Coach may need to help student steer when backing. Remember, the focus of lesson is on forming good habits of starting and stopping. The distances moved forward and backward may be increased as student improves.

7. Lesson 2 may be combined with this lesson for student who has had lessons in a school program.

8. Expect student and Coach to be a little nervous this first lesson. Don't hesitate to talk each other through the correct steps to put each other at ease. With plenty of patience and repetition, good progress will result. No loud voices, please.

9. Be alert for both of you becoming tired. Two short practice sessions are usually better than one long one at the beginning.

LESSON 2
MAKING LEFT AND RIGHT TURNS

In this lesson, students will learn how to use skilled steering methods, proper positioning, efficient eye habits, and proper speed control for making turns. They will be able to apply the traffic laws that will result in correct left and right turns. Turning at busy intersections will be reserved for advanced lessons.

STEERING WHEEL SKILLS

Hand Positions

Use the rim of the wheel. Hands should be placed palms down on the steering wheel's rim. Using the spokes or reaching under the rim may cause problems in straightening the car. Do not wear coats with large cuffs.

Use a firm grip. The grip on the steering wheel should be firm but not tight. A tight grip leads to fatigue and makes it more difficult to sense the "feel" of the wheel actions and road conditions.

Use a nine-three position. Picturing the steering wheel as the face of a clock, place your hands in the nine o'clock and three o'clock position for most normal driving. If your seat is adjusted properly, your arms should be bent so your hands can easily reach the top half of the steering wheel.

Center Steering

Center steering means keeping the car in a straight line down the center of the path. Only very small movements of the steering wheel are required for good lane control.

Slight Turn

Making a slight turn means turning the steering wheel about one-eighth turn to the right or left of center steer. For most cars, this will be about the right amount for a lane change.

8

Half Turn

 This is turning the steering wheel through one-half a circle or 180 degrees. To do this, start at the nine-three position and turn the steering wheel a half turn without lifting your hands off.

Full Turn

This involves turning the steering wheel as far right or left as it will go. This is about two complete turns for most cars. The hand-over-hand method is required.

Hand-Over-Hand Method

The hand-over-hand method of turning corners helps you make big, smooth hand movements. Avoid making small up-and-down hand movements on only the sides of the steering wheel. How quickly and how much you turn the steering wheel will depend upon both the speed of the car and the sharpness of the corner.

 To steer left, slip the right hand down to about the five o'clock position. Then push up and all the way around to the left side.

 As your left hand comes to the bottom of the wheel, remove it from the wheel and cross it over the top of your right arm.

 The left hand then grasps the top of the wheel and continues turning. As this is happening, the right hand comes off the bottom and is placed on the right side of the steering wheel. Continue as needed.

 To steer right, slip your left hand down to about the seven o'clock position. Then push up and all the way around to the right.

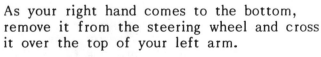 As your right hand comes to the bottom, remove it from the steering wheel and cross it over the top of your left arm.

 The right hand then grasps the top of the wheel and continues turning. As this is happening, the left hand is taken off the bottom and is placed on the left side of the steering wheel. Continue as needed.

When to Start Steering

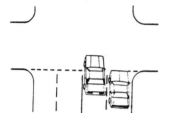

For most left turns, begin steering when your front door is about even with the edge of the intersecting roadway. For right turns, begin steering when the front of your car is about even with the edge of the intersecting roadway.

When to Straighten Front Wheels

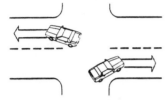

Just as the front end of your car reaches the lane into which you are turning, begin straightening the front wheels. You do this by releasing your grip on the steering wheel so as to allow it to slip through your fingers back to center steer. If you straighten too soon, the car will veer away for the intended pathway. If you begin straightening too late, no slipping will occur. Then, you must use quickly the hand-over-hand method in the opposite direction.

POSITION ON THE ROADWAY

Proper lane position is important at the beginning of the turn, during the turn, and at the end of the turn. Always stay in your own lane all the way around the corner. This lessens the chance for conflict with other vehicles. It also makes for a smoother and more efficient maneuver. Always signal well in advance of any lane change and turning maneuver.

Law Requirements

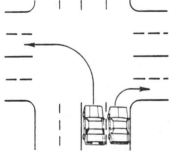

Traffic laws require that left turns be made from the lane farthest left in the direction you are going. Then turn left into one of the lanes going your direction. Right turns must be made from the lane farthest to right and into the first lane on the right side.

Spacing for Turns

When cars go around corners, the rear wheels make a new set of tracks inside those made by the front wheels.

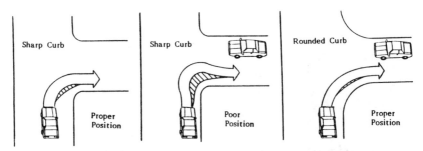

Therefore, the sharper the turn, the wider the pathway you will need. For rounded curbs, you should position your car about one-half car width from the curb before turning. For sharper curbs, position your car about one car width away from curb before coming to the corner.

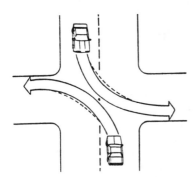

The space needed for most left turns will be just slightly more than the width of your car. The turning path should go just to the center of the intersection. This allows cars from the other direction to make left turns at the time you are turning left.

EYE HABITS FOR TURNING

Check All Four Corners

As you approach an intersection, scan all four corners for control signals, signs, and markings. Check the shape and sharpness of the curbing. Then, look two or more times down each side street for traffic.

Picture the Path to Take

As you reach an intersection, picture the full width and length of your turning path. Then, look ahead through the center of this travel path. As you start

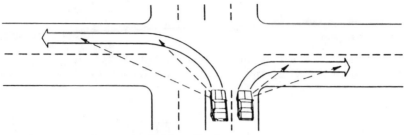

turning, continue to look all the way through the turn. This will help you follow the proper path and keep alert for other traffic. It will help you decide when to start straightening the front wheels. You will tend to steer toward where you look.

Make Mirror Checks

Make quick glances in the mirrors for the position of other traffic. For right turns, be alert for two-wheelers next to the curb. On left turns, be on the lookout for vehicles about to overtake and pass you.

SPEED CONTROL

After you have signaled to turn, slow down and start the positioning of your car. The proper speed for most turns is about ten to twelve miles per hour. Unless you are going uphill, use cover brake during the turn. Always be ready to yield to other vehicles and pedestrians.

Speed up slightly as the front of your car begins to enter the proper lane. This will help straighten the front wheels if you allow the steering wheel to slip through your fingers. Until you have some skill, go easy on the speed-up action.

USE OF MENTAL REHEARSAL

Making maneuvers in a car involves constant muscular coordination. This coordination must become an automatic process which can be called up by your will. You could acquire such coordination more quickly by using mental rehearsal before coming to practice. To use mental rehearsal, form a picture in your mind of the steps you are to follow. Then, you practice the maneuver in your imagination over and over again. This helps program your mind to provide your body with the proper message at the correct time. It will also help you identify and correct errors.

PUT IT ALL TOGETHER

1. *Check Traffic and Signal*
2. *Pick Proper Position.*
3. *Scan the Intersection.*
4. *Slow to Proper Speed.*
5. *Look Through Turn Path*
6. *Steer Hand-Over-Hand.*
7. *Straighten Front Wheels.*
8. *Speed Up Slightly.*

ACTIVITIES AND COACHING TIPS

1. The Coach should drive the car to a vacant level parking lot. On the way to the practice area, demonstrate and explain the proper steps for turning corners. Tell student when or where to start turning and how to straighten the front wheels for coming out of the turn. Have student watch your hands as well as the roadway.

2. On the parking lot, identify a rectangular area about 150 by 200 feet with plastic bottles or boxes filled with sand or dirt. This will allow for standard ninety degree turns. If a parking lot is not available, select a residential area with level streets and little traffic.

3. First, have student review the starting and stopping habit. Then, with selector lever in park and the motor idling, have student demonstrate the hand-over-hand method for turning. After this method is shown, have student start making left turns around the rectangular area very slowly. When needed, help out by saying, "start turning, hold, and start straightening." Coach should be ready to use left hand to assist. After a few left turns are made, practice some right turns.

4. As soon as a few turns are made, attention should be given to proper eye habits. Learning to picture the intended path and "looking through" the turn is the key to making smooth and correct turns.

5. After the student makes progress with steering wheel skills and eye habits, it is time to start practicing proper positioning and signaling on level streets in a quiet residential area. When on streets, the Coach must be "reading" the traffic picture around the car, and at the same time observing the driver's hand and feet movements. Be ready to assist.

6. The application of speed control is last. The timing of physical actions is closely related to the speed of the car. Introduce speed gradually during practices.

7. Beginners need to realize that the time to begin the straightening up process is when the front wheels, not the hood, start to point down the street being turned onto. Once a student can coordinate the controlled slipping of the steering wheel with a slight speed-up, they will get the front wheels to recover properly.

8. Progress to areas which provide turning from stopped and moving positions, at hill tops and at bottom of hills, at corners with both sharp and rounded curbs, and from a wide street to a narrow street. Gradually progress into areas with moderate traffic. The lesson may need at least three practice sessions.

In a moving vehicle with lives at stake, we will need to have habits and skills that pay off. The test of an expert driver comes in that split second when a problem situation comes up. It is then that well established habits will see her or him through safely.

LESSON 3
ENTERING AND LEAVING TRAFFIC

When entering or leaving traffic, you should prepare well in advance. Sudden actions create serious conflicts with other traffic. In this lesson you will learn the proper steps to take so you can prevent such conflicts. You will also learn how to park safely on hills. Such parking is usually required on state license exams.

ENTERING THE TRAFFIC STREAM

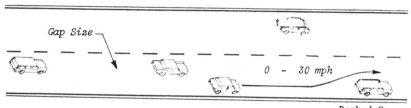

Signal

Move the signal light lever down as for a left turn. Use a light touch, moving the lever with the ends of fingers.

Check Traffic

Look forward to see that you have a clear path of travel. Then look in the mirrors and over your shoulder to check traffic to the sides. It is best to look both ways more than once to make sure you have not overlooked a vehicle that is coming out from a driveway. Bicyclists can be difficult to detect.

Select a Gap in Traffic

To enter traffic in town where the speed limit is thirty mph, you will need about an eight-second gap in traffic. Usually, this is a little more than one-half block. On rural roads, you will need at least a 15-second gap in traffic. These gaps will allow you time to yield the right-of-way.

Move and Steer Left

As soon as you have enough gap in traffic, look forward and speed up gradually. Look down the middle of your path.

15

Center Steer and Cancel Signal

As the front end of your car reaches the intended path, turn to center steer. Turn the signal light off.

LEAVING THE TRAFFIC STREAM

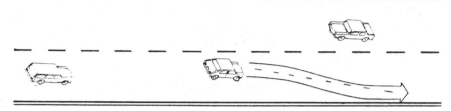

Select Proper Parking Place

Be sure to find a place that is legal to park. It is best not to park across from a driveway or another parked car. Check for high curbs and objects on either side of curbing.

Signal

In urban areas, signal at least 100 feet before steering toward the curb. In rural areas, signal 200 feet ahead.

Check Traffic

You should be checking forward and to the rear as you signal and start slowing down. Check both mirrors to make sure your signal has been seen. Check the blindspots.

Brake and Steer

Before braking, ease up on the gas pedal. Then, flash the brake lights by pumping lightly on the brake pedal. Steer into the pathway next to the curb.

Stop Parallel to Curb

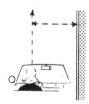

Beginners have trouble judging how close their car is to the curb. It is best to picture a path the width of your car next to the curb. Then, line up the middle of your car with the center of this path while "creeping" parallel to the curb. Your body should be about four feet from the curb.

DOWNHILL AND UPHILL PARKING

Turning the front wheels toward or away from the curb will prevent a car from rolling away if the park gear or brakes should fail. Some states require it on a hill.

Downhill

After stopping parallel to the curb, allow the car to creep forward slightly by releasing some pressure on the brake pedal. As the wheels begin to roll, turn the steering wheel quickly toward the curb. Stop just as the tires touch the curb.

Uphill

After stopping parallel to curb, place the selector lever in "N". Allow the car to creep backward by releasing some pressure on the brake pedal. Just as the car starts moving, turn the steering wheel sharply away from the curb. Stop just as the front tires reach the curb. Secure the car.

Remember

Select Place - Signal Early - Check Traffic

Brake and Steer - Stop Parallel - Turn Wheels

ACTIVITIES AND COACHING TIPS

1. Select a residential practice area so that the entering and leaving traffic skills can be combined with making left and right turns. Progress to streets with moderate traffic.

2. Find some hilly areas for practicing the up and down hill parking. In this lesson, the student should learn where the blindspots are around the car. Make sure proper mirror use and checks over the shoulder start to become a habit.

3. When you are selecting streets with moderate traffic, it is best to limit turning to right on and right off. Left turns against traffic are best left for the more advanced lessons.

LESSON 4
LANE POSITIONING AND SPEED CONTROL

Guiding and positioning a vehicle comes naturally to most people. Even so, one can improve this ability by learning good seeing habits and by getting a knowledge of what to expect from the car controls in response to the various actions taken.

In this lesson, students will learn how to check the mirrors and gauges without losing lane control. They will be able to identify the two-second following distance and the four-second stopping distance. Also, they will learn to downshift, to accelerate rapidly, and to recover from dropping off the edge of the pavement onto the shoulder.

EYE HABITS FOR STEERING

How well you can steer your car along a pathway will depend on how well you use your eyes. Here are three guidelines that can help you steer better.

Picture the Intended Path of Travel

First, you will need to get a picture in your mind of where you intend to go. When lanes are not marked, imagine a carpet the width of your car unrolling ahead.

Look Down the Middle of the Path

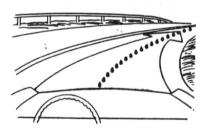

To guide your car, picture an imaginary line down the middle of your intended path. Looking up and down the center of your intended path provides the main point of reference toward which to steer. But, always keep your eyes moving.

If you are in doubt about your car's position in a lane, check your outside rear-view mirror. You should be able to see how far the left side of your car is from the road markings. Also, ask your instructor how close the side of your car is to the right edge of the road or lane line.

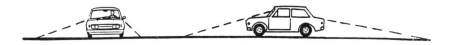

Realize that there is a large area of the roadway around the car that a driver cannot see. It will help to remember that your body is about two feet from the left side and four feet from the right side of your car. When space is quite limited on both sides, steer you car closer to the objects on the left side where the small distances are easier to judge.

Look Far Ahead

A safe driver should watch the road well ahead of the car to provide time to make decisions and have space for taking actions. The distance is called a visual lead. In town, you should be looking about one block ahead or a visual lead of about eight to twelve seconds.

MAINTAINING LANE POSITION

How to Make Steering Corrections

To guide your car along a straight path will require a slight movement of the steering wheel. These corrections redirect the car as it begins to drift away from the path. To help make corrections, imagine a line that runs down the middle of your car and stretches out in front. Then, you note when the car starts drifting off this imaginary pathway. To make the necessary corrections, move the steering wheel only about an inch or two at a time. If not, you will tend to oversteer and start weaving.

How to Check the Mirrors and Gauges

If you look away from the path of travel for any length of time, your car will tend to lose lane position. Thus, make a quick glance to one mirror or gauge at a time. Instead of making one long look, make two or three quick glances to get the information you need. Of course, you should pick the best time to look away from the roadway to make these checks.

 Check the fuel gauge to see if there is plenty of gasoline for your trip. It is best to keep the gas tank at least one-fourth full at all times.

 Check whether the battery is being charged or discharged. The pointer should stay about the center while moving. If a red light is used, it should go off after the motor is started. When a discharge shows while you are driving, go to the nearest service station to have it checked.

 Check the temperature gauge. A pointer or red light shows when the temperature of the motor coolant is too hot. When this happens, park and turn the motor off. Do not operate the car until the cause is located and corrected.

 Check the oil pressure. A red light or pointer shows when the oil pressure is below normal. If the light comes on while you are driving, pull over to park and turn off the motor. Do not operate your car until the problem has been corrected. Otherwise, costly damage results.

Positioning on Streets Without Markings

On most side streets and some rural roads, there are no lane lines. In such cases, you can estimate where the center is. You can also use your own body's position. If you are about one-third of the way from the right curb to the left curb, then your car should be in the middle of the right lane. On busier roads, there may be an oil slick down the middle of each side of the roadway. If so, then your body should be just to the left of the oil slick.

When driving along the side of parked cars, place your body about eight feet out from the side of these cars. If you meet an oncoming car in this situation, first make sure there is a pathway at least ten feet wide between the oncoming car and the parked cars. Then, steer toward the middle of this pathway. When in doubt, yield the right-of-way.

Here are some common errors to check out.

- Hugs left or right side of lane.
- Veers left to avoid roadside objects.
- Sits on edge of seat to see over hood.
- Mirrors are dirty or out of adjustment.
- Is not aware of speed.

OFF-ROAD RECOVERY

You may go off the road onto the shoulder accidently or on purpose. It's important to avoid steering back quickly onto the pavement. The edge of the pavement may be two to four inches above the surface of the shoulder. Turning quickly at high speed against this edge can throw your car out of control across the road into other traffic. Braking with two wheels on a soft shoulder and two wheels on the pavement can put your car into a skid. Don't panic, and follow these steps.

Center Steer

As soon as the two outside wheels are off the pavement, steer straight ahead and parallel with the edge.

Slow Down

Let up on the gas pedal. Do not use the brakes unless you are headed for a concrete bridge abutment or other such fixed object. If you must brake, use a slight pumping action so you can steer. Slow to about 30 miles per hour.

Signal and Turn Onto Pavement

Steer about one-fourth turn onto pavement. Straighten up into the first lane, and speed up to flow of traffic. Do not brake or steer quickly!

SPEED CONTROL SKILLS

Acceleration and Deceleration

Acceleration is the ability of a car to increase from one speed to a higher speed within a given period of time. Just pressing down on the gas pedal is the usual way to pick up speed. To pick up speed more quickly, downshift to a lower gear ratio. To downshift, let up on the gas pedal and shift the selector lever to "D-1" or "D-2". Then step on the gas pedal. Check the owner's manual.

Rapid acceleration can be obtained by quickly stepping on the gas pedal all the way to the floor. This results in a forced downshift and a quick pick up of speed. Such action may be needed for merging or passing.

Besides using the brake for deceleration, you can also slow down by downshifting. Continue to let up on the gas pedal after downshifting. "D-1" is used for speeds under 40 mph and shifting to "D-2" will allow for even a further decrease in speed. Be very careful when downshifting on slippery surfaces. Otherwise, the sudden speed change may cause the wheels to skid sideways.

Maintaining Steady Speeds

To keep a steady speed, you will need to make slight changes in the pressure on the gas pedal. Use a kind of squeezing action on the pedal. Even on level roads, speed control is almost a continuous task because of the wind and the surface conditions. It will help to make regular but quick glances at the speedometer. Also, learn to be sensitive to vehicle vibrations and noises, such as those of the tires, engine, and body.

An automatic speed control device, called cruise control, is available for most cars. Do not use this device in heavy traffic or on slick roads. Check the owner's manual.

Adjusting Speed for Following and Stopping

You will need a minimum distance of four seconds for stopping and two seconds for following other cars. The best way to measure these timed distances is to use the counting method. After counting out the distances a few times, you should be a good judge of how much space is needed for stopping and following. The following steps will help you get started.

First, pick a fixed checkpoint along the road ahead. This may be a sign, a tar strip, a light post, or any other fixed object.

 Second, start counting the seconds as soon as the rear end of the car ahead reaches your checkpoint. Count "one thousand and one, two thousand and two," and so forth.

 Third, when the front end of your car reaches the checkpoint, stop counting. If you reach the checkpoint before finishing the two-second count, you are following too closely.

ACTIVITIES AND COACHING TIPS

1. The best area to practice this lesson is a rural hard surfaced road with good sight distance, wide shoulders, and little traffic. Some streets at the edge of a community or suburb may be suitable. The student should be asked to review the steps for the off-road recovery on the way to area.

2. It will help the student to be told a few times how far the right side of the car is from the edge of the pavement. Coach should ask the driver where he or she is looking from time to time. To focus on looking far ahead does not mean one should not observe the hood sometimes to help with small corrections.

3. To help with eye movements, Coach should ask a few questions such as: "How much gas do we have? How much is the battery charging? How fast is the car going? What is the engine temperature? Is the oil pressure okay? Is a car following us?"

4. Have student practice holding the speed of car steady for some distance at 30 mph, 35 mph, and 40 mph. Ask student to compare the car noises for the various speeds. When meeting other cars at first, the Coach may wish to place his or her left hand on the lower part of the steering wheel. This can reassure the student of a readiness to help if needed. Beginners

may tend to focus on an oncoming vehicle rather than on the center of his or her own pathway.

5. Coach explains to the student how they will start practicing the off-road recovery exercise. Then, the student is asked to drive at about 35-40 mph. As the speed is reached, the Coach places his or her left hand on the bottom of the steering wheel. The Coach guides the car so that two wheels gradually drop off onto the shoulder while two wheels stay on the pavement. The student is then asked to follow the proper steps for making a recovery. After two or three trials at speeds no greater than 45 mph, the student is asked to do a drop off without Coach assistance. The Coach assistance is provided first because students too often may misunderstand the instruction and take all four wheels onto shoulder.

   A main objective of this exercise is to help the student become comfortable with going off and back onto the pavement. Then, there should be no hesitation for using the shoulder as an escape path. Do not practice this when shoulders are wet and soft.

6. Practice downshifting to "D-2" and "D-1". In each position, have student accelerate and decelerate. Then compare pick up and slow down with driving in "D". Practice rapid acceleration. Make sure traffic is not close by when practicing these skills.

7. Practice identifying the two-second following and the four-second stopping distances. Check out the twelve-second visual lead.

8. After traveling 40-45 mph on rural roads, students have a tendency to misjudge how much to slow down for turning right onto a side road. So, your student should be coached well ahead as to proper speed.

9. If there is a need to explain or discuss the proper steps to follow, don't hesitate to park along the side of the road. Practice using hazard lights. Always have the Handbook and Owner's manual available for review.

LESSON 5
CHANGING LANES IN TRAFFIC

On streets where there are two or more lanes going in one direction, you will need to change lanes in order to make turns or to park. Also, you will want to change lanes for better visibility, for an improved flow of traffic, and to avoid conflicts. Lane changes on multiple-lane streets usually take place at speeds of 30 mph or more. Therefore, in addition to learning simply the proper steps to follow, you should concentrate on developing good positioning and timing skills.

ADVANCE PREPARATION

Always begin planning a lane change well in advance of the point you wish to make such a maneuver. It does take time to make a thorough check of the conditions around your car. Also, the position of other traffic around your car could cause some delay. Try to avoid ever having to make a last minute lane change.

Check Roadway Conditions

You should develop the habit of scanning the roadway well ahead for your lane as well as the other lanes. Be alert for roadway width changes, blocked lanes, or surface conditions. Remember, certain right-of-way laws apply where a lane ends or is blocked. Also, you should not plan for a lane change where you would have to cross over a solid lane line.

Signaling for a lane change at or near an intersection could lead other drivers or pedestrians to expect a turning maneuver. Therefore, if you can't change lanes before reaching an intersection, you should not signal until your car has at least crossed the intersection.

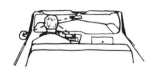

Check Traffic Conditions

 You will need to check out other traffic ahead, to your sides, and to the rear. Is there a clue that one of the other drivers is starting to enter the same lane you wish to enter? What about the driver waiting to turn into your street. Will this other driver pull out in front of you because he or she expected you to turn into the shopping center? Remember, it is hard for others to tell whether you are planning to make a turn or a lane change.

Maintain a Two-Second Following Distance

Always keep at least two seconds of distance behind the car ahead of you. This gives you better visibility, and provides enough space for you to cut back in case of an error.

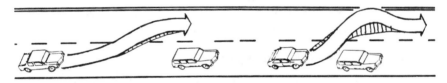

STEPS TO FOLLOW

Signal Well Ahead

Once you have decided to change lanes, signal well in advance of the point where the maneuver is to take place. Make sure the signal flashes five or six times before you start steering. This gives other drivers a better chance to see your signal and respond. In heavy traffic, another courteous driver may be able help you make the change.

The turn signal lever on most cars has a special way for indicating a lane change. You need to hold the signal lever only part way up or down to flash the turn lights. Then you just release the lever for the lights to go off.

Select a Safe Gap

You will need to identify a four-second gap in traffic in the lane you expect to enter. To do this, you must

make checks over your shoulder as well as mirror checks. Making checks over your right shoulder are very important when changing lanes from left to right. These checks must be quick glances. Otherwise, you might overlook a car in front that may be slowing down. Remember, you must still maintain good lane control and a steady speed while checking all around your car.

Check Your Blindspots

Before starting to move sideways, make one last over-the-shoulder check in the direction of lane change. This allows you to double check the blind spot for a safe gap. Checking over your shoulder to rear while maintaining good lane and speed control will take coordination and lots of practice.

Steer and Adjust Speed

As soon as you have double-checked your blind spot, start steering and increasing your speed slightly. Steering gradually allows you or other drivers to make adjustments in case of errors. As you reach the new lane, return to center steering and adjust your speed to that of the flow of traffic.

Cancel Signal

As soon as the lane change is completed, release or cancel your turn signal light.

Check traffic – Signal – Select gap – Check blindspot
Adjust speed – Steer – Cancel signal – Adjust speed

ACTIVITIES AND COACHING TIPS

1. The lesson will need to be conducted on multiple-lane streets or highways. Select a time when there is light to moderate traffic. Make sure your student is ready for traffic. First, review the two-second following distance.

2. Before making lane changes, have student practice making checks over the right and left shoulders for blindspots. Repeat until student can maintain good speed and lane control while making these checks. Beginning drivers usually have a tendency to start steering or slowing down before completing over-the-shoulder checks.

3. When making the first two lane changes to right and left, the student should be asked to count out loud five signal light flashes before steering. Remind the driver that making two or more quick glances to rear is better than one long look. Also, warn the driver that while checking to the rear, an ongoing vehicle could start slowing down for some reason.

4. After some practice in light traffic, a student should have the opportunity to practice changing lanes in moderate traffic at speeds up to 45 mph.

5. It is usually best to make right turns off and on the through streets or highways in this lesson. Wait for an advanced lesson for making left turns against traffic.

INTENDED PATH OF TRAVEL

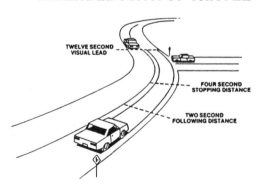

TWELVE SECOND
VISUAL LEAD

FOUR SECOND
STOPPING DISTANCE

TWO SECOND
FOLLOWING DISTANCE

LESSON 6
ANGLE PARKING AND TURNABOUTS

How to turn through various angles while backing is the new skill to be learned in this lesson. Proper positioning of the car for moving forward and backward in close quarters should be the focus of learning. Also, you may need much practice in making quick glances to front of your car while still keeping a good sense of where you are going as you continue backing.

Skills used for angle parking in driveways can be used for turning your car around. If you must turn around on a rural highway or a dead-end street with no driveways nearby, then you will want· to use the three-point turnabout. It is more hazardous, so you should use it only when necessary.

PARKING IN DRIVEWAYS

In residential districts, most people park in driveways. Entering and backing from a narrow driveway can be very hazardous. So, always move your car very slowly while making visual checks to all sides.

Entering a Driveway from the Left

Signal well in advance and check the mirrors for following cars. A driver may start to pass since your signal could be interpreted as a turn at the next intersection.

Start turning left just as the front of your car reaches the edge of the driveway.

Position your car to the side of the driveway that you intend to back out toward.

Entering a Driveway from the Right

Signal well in advance and check the mirrors. Be alert for two-wheeled vehicles. So, check over your shoulder to the right for the blindspot.

Keep at least one car width from the curb. For narrow driveways on an incline, you may need to swing out past the center line. When the traffic is heavy, pull over to the curb and wait for a gap.

Start turning right as soon as the front end of your car reaches the driveway. Position your car to the side of the driveway that will be easiest to back out from.

Backing Into a Driveway

When practical, consider backing into a driveway to park. Then, you can drive out forward with the best visibility to the right or left.

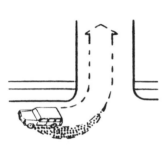

Signal, pull past the driveway, and stop along the curb about one-half car width away.

Check traffic to front and rear as the front end of your car may go out past the center of the street.

Steer sharp right as you creep backwards into the driveway.

Straighten the front wheels as the car passes the curb. Position in driveway as desired.

Backing from a Driveway to the Right

Back to the sidewalk, stop, and check traffic.

Looking over your right shoulder, back to curb, stop, and check traffic again. Make quick glances to front for clearance since the front end will swing to left.

Creep car slowly while steering a sharp right into the first traffic lane. As front end come into the street, straighten front wheels and come to stop. Go forward.

Backing from a Driveway to the Left

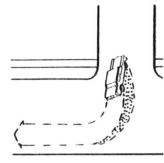

As you back up, make stops at the sidewalk and curb to check for pedestrians and traffic.

Creep until your front door reaches the curb. Steer left into the traffic lane across the street. Look over your left shoulder to guide your steering. But, keep glancing to right and front.

As your car becomes parallel with the curb, straighten the front wheels and come to a stop.

ANGLE PARKING SITUATIONS

When parking off-street in shopping centers, stay away from improperly parked and damaged vehicles. These may be clues to unskilled drivers. Parking next to a van or truck will limit your visibility. Also, be aware of the heat build-up inside a closed car. On a sunny day when the temperature is at least 80 degrees, the inside of a car can reach 130 degrees. Never leave children or pets locked up in a car on such a day.

Entering Acute Angle Parking Spaces

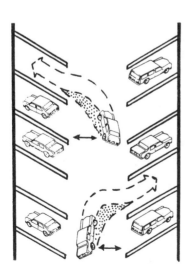

Signal, check traffic, and move to about one car width away from the parked cars on the side you wish to park.

When your front end passes the first line of the space, turn into the middle of the open space.

Straighten your wheels and pull into the space parallel with the lines. Creep forward until the front tires touch curb or your front end is even with the lines at end of space.

Open door to check if you are properly centered. If not, then reposition.

Entering Perpendicular Parking Spaces

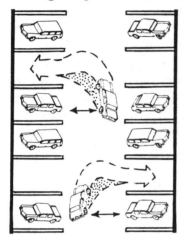

Signal, check traffic, and move as far away from the space as you can get.

When your front end reaches the center of the stall, start turning sharply for a full turn of the steering wheel.

Then pull forward and parallel with the lines.

Open car door to check if you are properly centered. If not, then reposition. Secure car.

Backing Out of Angle Parking Spaces

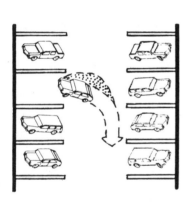

Check traffic and start creeping backward. All four corners of your car should be checked all during the maneuver.

Start steering slightly and allow your front end to come within two feet of the car to side.

As your front end clears the back bumper of other car, steer sharply in proper direction.

As your front end swings around, straighten and stop. Go ahead.

THREE-POINT TURNABOUT

This maneuver should not be attempted in traffic, near a curve, or at a hill where visibility is limited. Try to stop at a spot free of trees, poles, fire hydrants, or other fixed objects near the curb or ditch.

In urban areas, try to stay away from high curbs. The front end and rear end of most cars can extend at least two feet or more from the tires. Therefore, a high curb could easily damage some underneath part of your car if you did not stop in time.

Position One

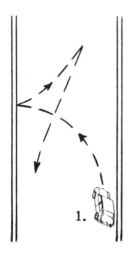

Check for traffic from both directions. Be especially alert for children who may be playing in the area.

Signal and pull over close to the curb and stop. Check traffic again.

Signal and creep forward while turning the steering wheel sharply left for a full turn.

Just before the front end of your car reaches the curb or ditch, straighten the steering wheel. It is easier to turn when the car is moving.

Stop just as the front wheels touch the curb or reach the ditch.

Position Two

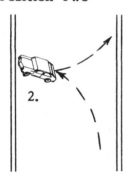

After stopping, shift to reverse and check traffic.

Look over your shoulder as you start creeping slowly and turning the steering wheel sharply to right for a full turn.

Just before the rear end of your car reaches the opposite curb or shoulder, start straightening the steering wheel. Then come to a complete stop.

Position Three

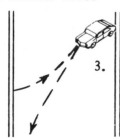

After you have stopped backing, shift to "D". Check traffic both ways.

Creep forward slowly so you will have time to steer left into the proper lane. If you cannot clear the curb or ditch, Back up to reposition your car and try again.

Note: When turning around in close quarters, the front wheels are straightened just before you stop to go in the opposite direction. This gives you a head start toward steering in the new direction.

ACTIVITIES AND COACHING TIPS

1. The Coach should demonstrate and explain how to back out and enter one's own driveway. Have student note when to start turning and when to start the straightening up process. Choose a very narrow alley or driveway on a grade to demonstrate special hazards and the need to check all four corners of the car. Then, demonstrate the three-point turnabout.

2. Start student practice in a residential area with little traffic. Pick an intersection where the streets are level and there is a clear view in all directions. Have student stop a short distance past one corner and parallel with the curb. Then, have student practice backing, very slowly, around each of the four corners. Most cars will move in reverse without pressure on the gas pedal. If so, use cover brake. When and how to straighten up while backing will take much practice. The Coach should be ready to help steer at first.

3. Pick a variety of alleys and driveways for the practice of entering and exiting. Finally, have the student try to enter and back out of her or his own driveway.

4. Student should drive to a shopping center or parking lot at a time when traffic is light. First, student should practice angle parking in spaces where no cars are nearby. Plastic gallon jars can be used to help identify the space. Next, practice parking beside only one vehicle. Then, practice parking between two cars.

5. On a narrow side street with low curbs, have student practice turning the car around by using the three-point method. This method may apply more to a rural road that has a bridge out or some other situation that would require turning around.

LESSON 7
IDENTIFYING CONTROLS AND HIGHWAY CONDITIONS

Students have learned the basic skills for controlling and maneuvering an automobile. Now it is time to learn efficient scanning habits for observing the traffic scene to the sides, the rear, and ahead. Within ten seconds, they should be able to identify those signs, signals, and pavement markings present. Also, they should be able to identify any changes in visibility, changes in space to the sides, and changes in traction ahead.

SCANNING HABITS FOR IDENTIFICATION

Habits for identification will be added to the three eye habits learned in lesson four. Constant scanning of the traffic scene will help drivers resist being distracted from the important events as well as prevent fixed stares.

Scan the Scene Ahead and to Sides

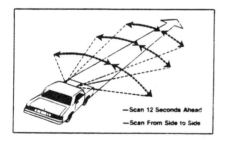

—Scan 12 Seconds Ahead
—Scan From Side to Side

Try to look a minimum of twelve seconds ahead of the car. This should give you time to identify and decide what to do about a hazard before your four-second stopping distance is reached. In cities, the twelve-second visual lead is about one block. In rural areas, it is about three-tenths of a mile at 55 mph. You can check this distance by glancing at the tenths digit on the odometer or you can count the seconds.

When you are behind other cars, look through the glass areas to the second and third cars ahead. Move to one side of your lane for a better view ahead. To scan from side to side, use the center of the intended path as the main point of reference. Then, make quick glances from the travel path to other areas and back again.

Scan the Road Surface

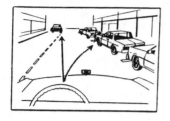

Watch the road surface with quick glances for pavement markings and changes in width. A shadow on the roadway could be a clue to a slick spot or another car ahead of the truck you wish to pass.

Get in the habit of making quick glances under parked cars for clues to pedestrians. Also, looking at the road surface beside a moving vehicle can help you judge its speed or a change in its direction.

Scan the Mirrors and the Dash

It is best to check the mirrors and dash at least every five seconds in urban areas and every ten seconds in rural areas. A mirror check is required the instant you observe a conflict developing ahead. Always check to see if your signals are being observed by others. Be sure to pick a safe time to look away from the intended path.

Scan by Large Groups

When there are many things to perceive, it is best to deal with them in a few meaningful groups. This aids in the selection process and helps insure that you do not overlook some important clues. All traffic information should be classified into three major groups. Search first for **traffic controls.** Search for **highway conditions** second. And third, search for **other user actions.**

Common Errors to Checkout

- Do you leave the signals on when not needed?
- Are you surprised by a car about to pass?
- Do you fail to notice conflicts in advance?
- Do you often have to make sudden stops?
- Do you fail to maintain space margins?
- Do you become easily distracted and tired?
- Have you had some near misses?

SEARCH FOR TRAFFIC CONTROLS

Traffic controls consist of laws and of devices such as signs, signals, and pavement markings. These devices have special shapes and colors to help you identify them quickly. They also have special symbols, word messages, or both. With only a few exceptions, the symbols should be read from the bottom up. Review your official state rules of the road as you practice drive.

Identify the Right-Of-Way Situations

In various situations, you must decide which vehicle or pedestrian should yield or be allowed to go first.

1. Entering unmarked or open intersections.

2. The lane ends or is obstructed.

3. Vehicles turning left across traffic.

4. Vehicles merging or exiting freeways.

5. Vehicles meeting emergency vehicles.

Identify Traffic Signs

1. Regulatory signs inform a driver of what must be done or what can't be done.

2. Warning signs inform drivers what changes to expect ahead such as roadway conditions, design features, and traffic conditions. They are yellow.

3. Guide signs provide drivers with directions to places and services. They include route markers.

4. Construction or Maintenance signs warn of temporary hazards ahead. Their color is bright orange.

Identify Traffic Signal Lights

Signal lights are provided to control traffic flow at certain locations. They indicate who has the right-of-way. You should have a clear understanding of what each color and symbol means. Expect green, yellow, and red arrows to be used more in the future. Learn the order that the lights flash on and off.

Identify Pavement Markings

Lines, symbols, and lettering are used with or without signs and signals. The words are read from near to those farther away. White lines are used to separate traffic going in the same direction. Yellow lines are used to separate traffic moving in the opposite direction. In general, broken lines permit being crossed over, and the solid lines restrict being crossed over.

SEARCH FOR HIGHWAY CONDITIONS

For safe control of a motor vehicle, highways should provide adequate space, visibility, and traction. **Space** is needed for crossing, turning, merging, or performing any other maneuver. Adequate space gives drivers better visibility, and gives them enough time to react to the changing conditions. How well drivers can guide their vehicles along a roadway will depend a great deal on **visibility.** Drivers must be able to see ahead and to all sides if they are to avoid collisions. **Traction** is the grip of the car's tires on the roadway. Without it, vehicle movement and control would not be possible. But, it is the **changes** in these conditions that drivers must identify and respond to well in advance.

Changes in Space to Sides

Less space to the sides of the car occurs when (a) the driver does not have at least one car-width of space next to the intended pathway, (b) there is less space available because of other traffic or objects like barricades, and (c) the roadway ahead gets narrower.

Here are some examples of space changes due to the highway features:

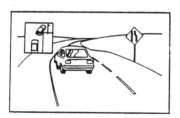

- Pavement width changes.
- Width of shoulder changes.
- Corner curbing is less rounded.
- There are embankments, posts, trees, snowbanks.
- There are rock slides or other objects on the roadway.

Here are some examples of space changes due to traffic conditions:

- Oncoming line of cars or parked cars, or both.
- Large vehicles turning.
- Double parked trucks.
- Bike riders and pedestrians.

Changes in Visibility

Good visibility depends on the sight distance ahead and a view to the sides. An area of less visibility is defined as a highway area in which the sight distance ahead or the view to the sides is less than that required for the safe travel at your present speed. This means, that without a speed adjustment, you would not be able to stop in time if another vehicle came into view.

Shrubs, buildings, signs, and embankments can block your view of private driveways and intersections. Hills, curves, and dips in the roadway can easily hide a slow moving vehicle or a disabled car. Be alert for mail boxes, telephone lines, and clouds of dust which could be a clue to the possible presence of pedestrians, animals, or other vehicles.

Other traffic can create visibility changes as well as space problems. Large trucks and busses can reduce your sight ahead and view to the sides. Vehicles turning or waiting to turn can cause reduced visibility too.

Changes in Traction

You must always be alert for areas of less traction. These areas can occur when the roadway conditions ahead lessen the friction or grip between the tires and the driving surface. It can seriously affect car control.

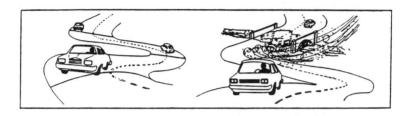

It is important to note whether the roadway is banked, crowned, or flat. Concrete usually provides for better traction than blacktop or brick pavements. Be alert for chuck holes, railroad tracks, and sewer covers. Also, identify whether the shoulder is below the level of the pavement.

Sand, mud, gravel, and wet leaves can cause skidding. Water, frost, ice, oil, snow, and tar also reduce traction. Spillage from trucks and dead animals could become a problem for car control. Remember, wind gusts, the bright sun, and changes in temperature can affect the surface conditions or the materials on the pavement.

COMMENTARY DRIVING

Commentary driving is a method for checking out how well a driver or passenger can identify all the events and clues happening around the car. It consists of making comments about whatever you see in the traffic scene around you while driving. You simply read aloud the traffic picture as it unfolds. Once you practice this method a few times, you will find it very helpful.

The method will be helpful because it forces you to identify things quickly and in advance of your car. You then will have a better idea as to whether you are seeing events in time to take proper actions. It also gives you a chance to compare your observations with those of others. Are you really developing selective seeing habits?

As you make comments, try to describe everything that could affect your path of travel. This includes what you see in front, to the sides, and in your mirrors. Your general pattern of comments should be related to such questions as, "What is it?" "Where is it?" "What is it doing?" If its condition is important, then include that in your comments.

Since proper timing of vehicle movement is one of the keys to safe driving, you will need to make comments of the events well ahead of your car. Obviously, you can't identify and comment on everything you observe. Therefore, comment first on what you think could be most likely to affect your intended path of travel.

It is best to begin with one group at a time. For traffic controls, you might make such comments as: "Open intersection...Speed limit is 35...My speed is 40... Signal light is stale green...Walk light just flashed off... My lane must turn left...No turn on red...Must yield to van...On a state highway...No passing zone."

Here are some examples for highway conditions: "No shoulder...Curve is flat...Blind intersection...Less space... Rough pavement in front of motorcyclist...Gravel on pavement...Divided highway ends."

Comments on other user actions may include such as: "Following car is tailgating...Truck is about to pass...No eye contact with child bicyclist...Parked car is backing... Oncoming car drifting toward center...Car is closing from right...Pedestrian is off curb...Van may not complete the turn...Ongoing car is braking."

After some practice with each group, try a running commentary on all groups. Comments then can evolve into statements such as: "No changes in roadway...No signal lights...Ongoing car OK...Parked cars on left OK... Intersecting car OK...Pedestrians OK." In urban areas, at the beginning of each block, you can say whether the intended path is clear or not clear. This shows that all the various clues have been checked out and there is no evidence for a problem within the next twelve seconds.

Tell what it is--Tell where it is--Tell what it is doing

ACTIVITIES AND COACHING TIPS

1. Before this practice session begins, have your student practice commentary driving as a passenger. Review the laws related to traffic controls.

2. Find a few through streets with a variety of traffic controls and roadway conditions. Try to find situations where there are changes in space to sides due to parked vehicles or in widths of the streets.

3. First, have the student drive up and down through streets with good lane and speed control. Focus on practicing the three scanning habits. So, keep turns and lane changes to a minimum. The Coach should demonstrate commentary driving from time to time.

4. Have a friend or relative ride in the middle of the back seat so he or she can watch the rear view mirror. This person should note whether the driver is moving his or her eyes to check the mirrors and dash at least once each block.

5. After the student becomes comfortable driving in traffic on through streets, have him or her do some commentary driving. Have comments made about traffic controls only at first. Then, have comments made only about highway conditions. Finally, have comments made about both traffic controls and the highway conditions.

6. This lesson and the next are critical to the development of those perceptual skills required for safe driving. Repeated practice in a variety of situations will pay off in the future.

Good habits are hard to acquire but easy to live with. Bad habits are easy to acquire but hard to live with. When you choose a habit, you also choose its end result. The best way to change a habit is to replace it with a new one.

LESSON 8
IDENTIFYING OTHER USER ACTIONS

Identifying and interpreting the actions of other users is one of the more difficult things you must do as a driver. Other highway users can travel at high speeds and make sudden changes in direction. They can start and stop very quickly. Therefore, the more evidence or clues you can discover about other users, the better you can predict if they are likely to move into your intended path of travel and cause a conflict.

In this lesson, you will learn to search for clues to the probable actions of automobile drivers, motorcyclists, bicyclists, and pedestrians. Included will be the kind of errors to expect from each highway user.

CLUES TO PROBABLE CONFLICTS

To avoid collisions, your primary search of the traffic scene must be directed toward those other user actions that could result in conflicts within your intended path of travel. The chance for other users to move into your twelve second path of travel will be called a conflict probability.

Evidence for and Against Conflicts

The best way to identify a conflict probability is to collect evidence (clues) for or against the conflict taking place. If you can find little of no evidence for another user to move into your twelve-second path, then you would identify that user as having a **low conflict** probability. A pedestrian walking away from the street or a parked car with no driver would be good examples. In another case, you judge that an intersecting car will cross your path up ahead. But, it will be at least twelve seconds away.

Other users may be identified as having more evidence for a conflict to take place than there is against such a conflict. Then, the users will be identified as having a **high conflict** probability. If there is some doubt as to such a conflict,

43

it is safest to assume the worst and predict a probable conflict. For example, a parked car with a driver, the front wheels turned out, and smoke coming from the exhaust should be called a high conflict probability.

Kinds of Evidence

As you are searching for evidence of probable conflicts, it will help to know what general things to look for. You may use the following questions to guide your search.

What and who is it? The type and size of a vehicle should help remind you of its various capabilities and limitations. A car with dirty windshields and bent fenders could be a clue as to the other driver's habits. The age of the driver may be important.

Where is it? This question will remind you to look for the position of another user on the roadway or within a lane. Also, you may expect certain traffic patterns in a residential or rural area that you would not expect in a business district.

What is it doing? You should be alert to the kind of maneuvers another driver is attempting. Try to determine if there is adequate space or time for the maneuver to be completed. Try to find out what another driver may do when faced with areas of less space, less traction, or less visibility.

What errors can be expected? Few collisions happen that don't involve a human error. Search for and expect pedestrian and driver errors. Look for clues that a traffic law may not be obeyed. Most errors involve the speed and right-of-way laws.

SEARCH FOR AUTOMOBILE CLUES

Type and Condition of Vehicle

Large trucks, buses, and motor homes take up more space when they are turning. They have reduced pick-up and braking. Body styles can create visibility problems. City buses may expect the right-of-way or take it.

Taxicabs may be in a hurry and take more chances. Drivers of high performance cars and sport models may make quick stops, starts, and cornering maneuvers. The economy compacts usually have reduced pick-up.

HIGH OR LOW PERFORMANCE

IMPROPER — OR OVERLOADED

Bent fenders and body damage could indicate a poor driver. Out-of-state license plates may be a clue to a driver unfamiliar with the road. Glass areas partially covered with ice, snow, dirt, or clothing will create a visibility problem. An improperly or overloaded vehicle can cause steering and braking problems.

Clues to Changes in Direction

Is the car in a passing lane? A turning lane? Next to curb? On the shoulder? Is the car centered in the lane or drifting to the edge of lane? What's the direction of the front tires? Are turn lights on? How long have they been on? What about the back-up lights, the brake lights, and the flasher lights?

Clues to Changes in Speed

A quick puff of smoke on a moving car indicates a change of speed. A rapid speed up will cause the back end to squat. The front end noses down with a quick stop. What about body lean on a turn?

SEARCH FOR DRIVER CLUES

Age and Condition

Older persons may be confused or slow to react. Younger persons may be inexperienced and take more chances. A short person may have a sight problem. A driver may be impaired.

Activity of Driver

Is the driver distracted by talking, smoking, eating, map reading, or window shopping? Has the driver made

eye contact? What kind of maneuver is being attempted?
Is there adequate space and time?

Common Errors to Expect

Fails to yield...Fails to adjust
speed...Fails to signal...Fails to
use proper lane...Stops or swerves
quickly to avoid objects.

SEARCH FOR MOTORCYCLIST CLUES

Age and Condition

Young persons may be inexperienced. Lack
of a helmet or goggles could affect vision.
Passenger may affect control. Improper
clothing may indicate a willingness to take
high risks.

Location and Activity

Is it close to curb, in middle of lane
or to one side of lane? Is it weaving,
turning, or stopping? What is the
condition of the pavement ahead of
of the cycle? Are two or more
cycles traveling together? Does the
driver and passenger lean on curves?

Common Errors to Expect

Turn signals are left on...Rolls through
stop sign...Rides on grease strip down
center of lane...Does not choose best
path to be seen by others...Rides in the
blindspot of car drivers...Makes quick
lane changes without warning.

SEARCH FOR BICYCLIST CLUES

Age and Condition

Children may lack knowledge of traffic laws. They
may be playing. A rider may be impaired. The bike
may lack fenders and reflectors.

Type and Size of Bike

Is the bike too small or too large for the rider? Is it a racing, multiple speed, or play bike? Is it properly equipped for riding at night?

Location and Activity

Is it close to curb, in the middle of a lane, or on a sidewalk? What is the condition of pavement ahead of the bike? Is is weaving, turning, or parking? Are there several in a group?

Common Errors to Expect

Rolls through stop sign...Does not signal...Rides facing traffic...Not aware of traffic behind...Uses improper lane...Does not have proper equipment and clothing for the operation of bike at night.

SEARCH FOR PEDESTRIAN CLUES

Age and Condition

Children are easily distracted and lack a knowledge of laws and vehicle capabilities. Older persons may be impaired or be a non-driver. What's a white cane mean?

Location and Activity

Is the person on sidewalk, on curb, or in the street? Is person standing, walking, or running? Where is the person looking? Is the person entering or exiting from a vehicle?

Common Errors to Expect

Darts out between cars...Walks when drunk...Crosses against signal lights... Fails to make eye contact.

SUMMARY

1. Search Drivers, Motorcyclists, Bicyclists, and Pedestrians for Clues to Probable Actions.

   a. Age and Condition.
   b. Location and Activity.
   c. Common Errors to Expect.

2. Search Motor Vehicles for Clues to Conflicts.

   a. Type and Condition.
   b. Changes in Direction.
   c. Changes in Speed.

3. Identify Other User Probabilities for Conflicts within your Twelve-Second Path of Travel.

   a. Evidence for Low Conflict Probability.
   b. Evidence for High Conflict Probability.

4. Become a Traffic Detective.

ACTIVITIES AND COACHING TIPS

1. When riding as a passenger in the family car, student can be asked to do commentary driving for short periods of time. Have student compare his or her observations with those of driver.

2. Review practice driving on the through streets used for the last lesson. Then, select additional streets with moderate traffic. The Coach should demonstrate what is to be identified by using commentary driving.

3. Have student use commentary driving for identifying the probable actions of other users.

4. This lesson can be combined with the next lesson.

Evaluation is most conducive to

learning when it provides for and

encourages self evaluation.

LESSON 9
POSITIONING AND TIMING AT INTERSECTIONS

In the first eight lessons, students have learned how to control the car and perceive those events taking place in and along the intended path of travel. Now it is time to learn how to respond safely to those situations identified. In this lesson, students will learn how to manage space and time at multiple-lane intersections. The main focus will be on making left turns against traffic.

SCANNING HABITS FOR INTERSECTIONS

Search for Traffic Controls

..Are signal lights about to change?

..Is there a "no turn on red" sign?

..Are there left turn only signs or signals?

..What controls do other drivers have?

..Are all lane lines white?

..Are some lanes for one direction only?

Search for Roadway Conditions

..Is there less traction due to worn surfaces?

..Are there surface materials? Is there poor visibility?

..Does the road width change across the intersection?

..What is the shape and sharpness of the curbing?

..Are there islands to channel turning movements?

Search for Other Traffic Conflicts

..Is the car behind tailgating?

..Is a truck hiding other cars?

..Will pedestrians delay the turning movements?

..Is a car speeding up to beat the light change?

..Is a parked car at the end of the block about ready to move into traffic?

POSITIONING AT INTERSECTIONS

Select the proper lane well in advance of the solid lane lines to avoid a serious conflict. Center your car within the lane and allow for a margin of space to each side. When stopping behind other vehicles, allow a space margin of about five feet. Then you will have plenty of room to stop should the ongoing vehicle stop suddenly after starting to move ahead.

Crossing Intersections

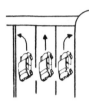 When crossing an intersection, make sure you do not get into a turn-only lane. If there are three or more lanes going your direction, choose the middle lane. If you have only two lanes in your direction, the right lane is the best unless left turns are not allowed.

Making Right Turns

 Right turns should always be made from the farthest lane to the right and into the lane farthest right. Depending on the sharpness of the curb, keep about one-half car width from the curb. Be alert for two-wheeled vehicles trying to squeeze by on the right side. Also, check for parked cars moving.

Making Left Turns

Left turns should be made from the lane farthest left going in your direction. Then turn into the first lane that is going your direction. If left turns are allowed from more than one lane, stay in the same lane all the way around. Make quick mirror checks for conflicts.

When making a left turn against traffic, pull into the intersection and establish your position just before you reach the lane you wish to turn into. Keep the wheels at center steer until the turn can be made. Otherwise, a following car could push you into the line of oncoming traffic. Allow enough space ahead for the oncoming car to make a left turn in front of your car. Be sure to make quick glances at the signal lights. You must be ready to clear the intersection when the yellow light comes on.

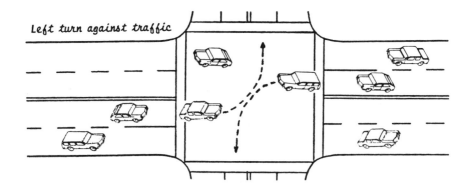

Left turn against traffic

TIMING AT INTERSECTIONS

Once you have selected the proper lane, you must then decide the best time to start crossing or turning. This involves choosing a safe gap in traffic. The gap in traffic is the distance or time between the back end of one car and the front end of the next car in line.

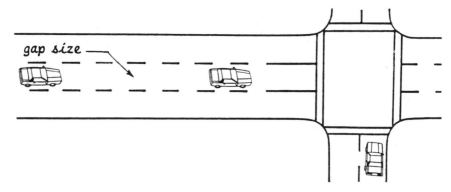

gap size

Choose the Best Time for Crossing

Crossing most intersections from a stopped position takes about four seconds, So, you should have at least a five-second gap in traffic before starting to move. Poor traction or visibility problems may be factors in the starting time.

Choose the Best Time for Turning

Right and left turns at a city intersection will usually require a minimum of six seconds to complete. So, you will need a gap in traffic of at least seven seconds. This is usually a little more than a half block for vehicles traveling 30 miles per hour.

ACTIVITIES AND COACHING TIPS

1. Route selection can begin by including some of the same situations used in the last two lessons. Then, it is well to proceed to unfamiliar situations so that the identification and decision-making skills can be integrated into one mental process. Crossing, turning onto, and turning off of busy through streets should lead to many of the situations which will require the desired responses. A variety of multiple-lane intersections are needed for the practice of positioning, gap selection, and left turns against traffic.

2. Right turns in traffic create little problem, and your student should have had considerable practice with them in the last two lessons. Therefore, this lesson should be devoted mostly to a variety of left turn situations that includes one-way streets, multiple-lane undivided streets, and divided highways when available.

3. Rather precise times for crossing and turning at intersections are recommended in this lesson. This is for the purpose of communication between Coach and the student during the training period. Eventually, drivers develop their own judgments of space relationships, so they no longer have to rely on such a counting method except as a check up from time to time.

4. Have student use a stop watch to find out the time it takes to cross or make turns at several different intersections. Compare these with those in your Manual. This can be done when standing at a corner or as a passenger in a car.

LESSON 10
MEETING AND FOLLOWING OTHER USERS

Other users can become a conflict by entering the driver's path of travel from the front, the rear, or either side. In this lesson, students will learn how to choose the proper position and speed to take for these conflicts once they have been identified. Then, they will learn how to communicate and time their actions in order to avoid the probable conflicts.

MAINTAIN ADEQUATE SPACE MARGINS

An adequate space margin must be provided at all times for braking, changing speed, and steering movements. It also provides for good visibility and swerving space. Picture the space margin as an imaginary protective space that extends to all sides of your car.

Allow at Least Two or Four Seconds Ahead

Under normal conditions, the two-second following distance and the four-second stopping distance provide minimum distances ahead. If you are behind a motorcyle or large truck, it is best to increase the following distance. Reduced traction always calls for an increase in stopping and following distances.

Allow at Least Two-Seconds Distance to the Rear

The distance to the rear is hard to control. If cars are following too closely (tailgating), allow more space ahead. Encourage them to pass.

Allow One Vehicle Width On At Least One Side

The distances to the sides should be enough to provide for errors in judgment and to provide for an "escape" path. When it is not possible to have one vehicle width of space to one side, allow more space in the front.

CHOOSE BEST PATH TO MEET AND FOLLOW

General Rules for Choosing the Best Path

- Which path is illegal to use?

- Which path has the best visibility?

- Which path has the best roadway surface?

- Which path has the most clear space to the sides?

- Which path has the best flow of traffic?

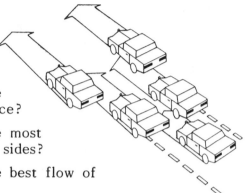

Choose the Best Path on Multiple-Lane Roadways

- On four-lane undivided or divided highways, it is best to keep right except to pass or turn. Many states require keeping to the right.

- On city streets with parked cars, it is best to avoid using the right lane except to turn right.

- When following other vehicles, move to one side of your lane to get a better view ahead. Get into the habit of looking around, through, and under other motor vehicles.

Choose the Best Path at Curves and Hills

- Enter a curve to the right next to the center line. This gives a better view and allows you to have more distance from the center line at the sharpest point of the curve.

- For a curve to the left, enter closest to the edge of the pavement for the best view. Try not to meet a vehicle at the sharpest part of the curve.

- When approaching a hillcrest, keep closest to the right edge of the pavement, and look for an escape path if needed.

Choose the Best Path for Hazards to the Sides

- When approaching side roads or driveways with visibility problems, move over at least one-half car width.

- When approaching a car parked on a shoulder, move over at least one-half car width.

- Remember, cars will use slightly more than one lane width as they enter and leave most parallel parking places.

Choose the Best Path for Surface Conditions and Weather

- Keep far right when driving through fog, smoke or a blinding rain.

- Try to avoid a shaded area on a cold morning and pot holes at any time.

- Crosswinds can push vehicles sideways. So, when approaching such areas, keep to that side from which the crosswinds are coming.

CHOOSE THE BEST SPEED TO MEET AND FOLLOW

Because speed is such a relative thing, deciding how fast to go calls for good judgement. If speed is too fast for conditions, the driver will be unable to stay on the intended path of travel or stop in time to avoid a crash. The high speed capability of a car should be considered only as reserve power for an emergency. Fast driving on public highways is not the mark of an expert driver. Skill comes in learning how to adjust speed for the constant changes in the road and traffic conditions.

Drivers cannot control road conditions and the movements of other traffic. But, drivers can control their own actions and the movement of their own vehicles by timing. Such timing requires proper speed adjustments.

Adjust Speed for Timing Situations

- Drivers should try to avoid meeting large vehicles at areas of reduced space such as bridges.

- Drivers should try to avoid meeting other vehicles opposite hazards such as bicyclists and children playing.

- Drivers should try to avoid meeting other vehicles at slippery areas such as shady spots and frost on bridges.

- Drivers should try to avoid meeting other vehicles opposite areas with strong crosswinds.

- Drivers should choose the best time for maneuvers, especially changing lanes and passing other vehicles.

- Drivers should time such actions as checking the mirrors, signalling, downshifting, adjusting the radio, and scenic viewing.

- Drivers should allow plenty of time for perceiving and responding to traffic controls. They should adjust speed for timed signal light changes.

Adjust Speed for Proper Following Distances

Increase the distance for certain **vehicle types.** Keep farther behind large trucks, campers, and buses which will block your view ahead and take longer to stop. Keep an increased distance from two-wheelers and sports cars.

Increase the distance for certain **traffic conditions.** In heavy traffic without adequate swerving space to either side, stay further back. Keep a greater distance from any car ahead that is tailgating any other car ahead. Any vehicle that is about tô turn should require a greater distance because it may not be able to complete the maneuver as expected.

Increase the distance for **adverse road conditions.** Less traction due to rain, snow, ice, loose gravel, or dirt all call for increased following distances. Pot holes and rough surfaces also lessen traction.

Increase the distance for your **own condition.** When you are not feeling well and must drive, keep a greater following distance because of slowed reactions.

Adjust Speed for the Kinds of Traffic

Choose a reasonable and proper speed for the **type of traffic** present. Is traffic heavy? Are there many trucks school buses, two wheelers, or pedestrians present? During late afternoon hours, drivers may be tired and in a hurry to get home. Late at night, drivers may be sleepy or under the influence of alcohol.

Choose the **common speed** of traffic. The larger the difference in speed of moving vehicles, the greater chance there is for conflicts and errors in judgement. Blending with the flow of traffic also saves gasoline.

Avoid driving in a **blindspot.** 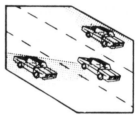 adjust your speed to move ahead or behind cars to either side so that you do not stay in any car's blind- spot for any length of time. Also, make sure no vehicle remains in your blindspot.

Avoid driving in **bunches.** Since there is more chance for conflict, adjust your speed to either work through the group or slow down and remain behind. If you must drive side by side with other vehicles during the rush hour traffic, allow an increased distance ahead.

Adjust Speed for Changes in Highway Conditions

Adjust speed for changes in **visibility.** A driver needs a clear, unobstructed view of the road ahead. Always adjust your speed so that your sight distance ahead is greater than your stopping distance. Remember, if you can't see cars on the side road, they can't see you.

Adjust speed for changes in the **space to sides.** When you are approaching an area of limited space to both sides with no swerving space, a speed adjustment is your only choice. Remember, the closer you must drive to objects and other users, the smaller the error in judgment that is needed to cause a problem. In such cases, the faster you go the less chance you have for making corrections.

Adjust speed for changes in **traction.** The amount of traction varies a lot with the conditions of the road sur- ace. There is little difference in traction for the types of paved roads when they are dry. But, what is on the surface of the pavement is what causes a change in the amount of traction. For example, wet roads can double the stopping distance of most cars.

Adjust speed for **curves.** When approaching a curve, adjust speed to the sharpness of the curve. Then, maintain a slight pressure on the gas pedal for better traction around the curve.

Adjust speed for **hills.** When approaching a hill, increase speed to gain enough momentum to reach the top without the need to increase speed again. If the pavement is 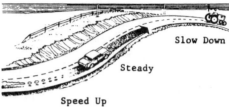 slippery, use a very gentle pressure on the gas pedal to avoid fishtailing. At the hillcrest, slow down slightly and be alert for slow moving vehicles. If the downhill is very steep or slippery, be prepared to downshift to help prevent your car from increasing too much momentum.

CHOOSE THE BEST COMMUNICATION

Whenever you plan to change position or speed, other users should be told in advance. There are many times when just your presence should be communicated. Communicating means exchanging information with others. It means receiving as well as giving information. As a driver, you will need to know if your signals are being received and heeded.

These are the methods for communicating:

Use Electric Signals.

You have a choice of turn signals, brake lights, back-up lights, or four-way flashers.

Use Body Actions.

You can choose to use hand signals, nod your head, smile, or just look confused.

Use the Horn.

Choose a gentle tapping, a sharp blast, or a steady blow of the horn.

Use the Headlamps.

You can flash your headlamps off and on or switch from low beam to high beam and back again.

Use Vehicle Position.

Drifting toward the lane line could indicate a readiness to change.

SUMMARY

To meet and follow other users, choose the best

Position – Time – Speed – Communication.

ACTIVITIES AND COACHING TIPS

1. Some of the practice areas picked for the last two lessons may be used. Try to include situations which include changes in space to sides, visibility, and traction. Also, select two-lane rural roads with plenty of hills, curves, and traffic. Review the 2-4-12 timed distances.

2. Choosing the best place to time the meeting of on-coming cars can begin in residential areas where parked cars can provide situations for reduced space. The simpler the situation to begin with, the better the timing concept can be applied. Narrow bridges, and narrow shoulders on rural roads can provide additional situations.

3. The student can be asked to explain the reason for lane selection and positioning within a lane. He or she should demonstrate speed adjustments for the changes in roadway conditions.

LESSON 11
MERGING AND EXITING AT INTERCHANGES

Interchanges are a unique feature of the highway system. They help make freeways and expressways the safest of all highways. This is because they eliminate intersections, signal lights, and they separate traffic going in opposite directions.

In this lesson, you will learn the proper steps for entering and exiting freeways. Once on the freeway, you can practice the guidelines learned in the last lesson for driving on multiple-lane roadways.

TYPES OF INTERCHANGES

There are two basic types of interchanges with several variations. Because of the shapes, one is called a diamond interchange and the other a cloverleaf interchange. Both provide for turning movements on and off the freeway from all four directions.

Diamond Interchange

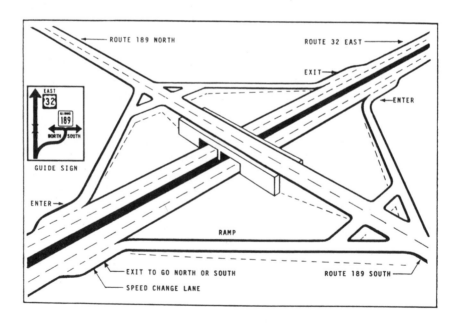

Interchanges are made up of ramps and speed change lanes. The ramps are short one-way roads that connect the two highways of different grade levels. They are usually designed for a speed of 35 mph. The speed change lanes are special lanes next to the main traveled lanes of the freeway. They make it possible to pick up speed for merging and to slow down for exiting. Speed change lanes are also called acceleration and deceleration lanes.

Cloverleaf Interchange

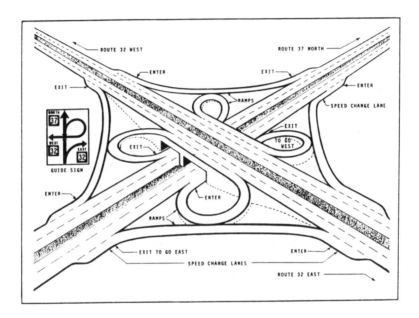

MERGING ONTO A FREEWAY

When entering a freeway from a ramp, you will be merging with high speed traffic. Merging is a maneuver in which the drivers of both vehicles are required to adjust speed and position. It is a coming together or blending of vehicles so that the flow of traffic remains smooth. Drivers, both on the freeway and ramp, have the responsibility of cooperating with each other. Here are the steps to follow for merging with high speed traffic.

Identify Proper Ramp

Observe the guide signs well in advance so you can identify which lane and ramp to take. Remember, ramps are one-way and backing up is a no no. You should know the route and direction you wish to go. Also, it is a good idea to know the name of a city or two in this same direction.

Pick a Safe Gap

When on the ramp, begin scanning for traffic on the freeway. You will need at least a four-second gap. Pick a gap that is far enough back so you will be able to reach the merging area about the same time as the lead vehicle. Be prepared with a second gap if the first one does not work out. Don't forget to keep a proper space margin from the other vehicles on your ramp.

Adjust Speed and Signal

As the ramp begins to flatten out and you approach the speed change lane, pick up speed. When you reach the speed change lane, signal a lane change and adjust your speed to that of the freeway traffic. Keep scanning and using your mirrors. Note the length of the speed change lane that is available.

Merge With Traffic

Continue to adjust your speed and position in order to join with the fast moving traffic in the gap you picked. Then, cancel your signal. Usually, you can expect vehicles on the freeway to change lanes and let you in.

Identify Ramp - Pick Gap - Signal - Speed Up - Merge

EXITING FROM A FREEWAY

Plan your exits well in advance. A last second exit can lead to a serious conflict. If you miss an exit, you may have to drive twenty or more miles out of your way. Here are the steps to follow.

Identify Exit

Most freeways will provide you with exit information one or two miles in advance. Be sure you know the route and direction to take. The diamond interchange has only one exit for both directions. The cloverleaf interchange has two exits (A–B), one for each direction.

Select Proper Lane

Guide signs will indicate the proper lane to select well in advance of the exit. Most exits will be made from the far right lane. The others are usually made from the far left. Keep track of the traffic around you at all times.

Enter Speed Change Lane Early

Signal and pull into the speed change lane as soon as you reach it. Then start slowing down. It is best not to slow down much on the lanes of the freeway. If there is no speed change lane, then reduce your speed gradually on the freeway. Flash your brake lights as a warning.

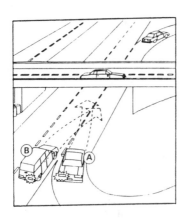

On the cloverleaf interchange, some of the speed change lanes are to be used for both entering and exiting traffic. These situations may result in traffic crossing each other's pathways. It can be difficult to time since one vehicle is slowing down while the other is speeding up. It is usually best to allow the entering driver to cross first.

Enter Ramp at Posted Speed

Always check your speedometer to make sure of your speed. Entering the ramp faster than the posted speed can be a serious mistake. Having to brake hard on a narrow curving roadway can lead to loss of control. This is especially true when the pavement is slippery.

Identify Exit--Select Lane--Signal--Adjust Speed--Enter

ACTIVITIES AND COACHING TIPS

1. The ideal area would be to have at least one diamond interchange and one cloverleaf interchange a short distance apart. A belt line road around a city usually makes for a suitable practice area. Where no interchanges are available in the immediate community, consideration should be given to planning a trip to a nearby area with interchanges.

2. As the car is driven to the practice area, have student review and discuss the proper procedures. A student may be reluctant at first to accelerate enough, so some coaching may be required. It is best to give a route number and direction so the student can get practice interpreting guide signs and selecting the proper ramp to enter for a given destination.

3. At a cloverleaf interchange, the student can first be directed to drive around all four ramps before merging onto the expressway or freeway. This way the student can get used to the ramp configuration and procedures to follow. It can serve as a kind of drill. It also shows a student how to turn around to go in the opposite direction on a freeway.

4. When exiting, have student assume he or she is on a trip. Then, give directions such as, "We are heading north and want to go west on route 40," or "We want to go west to Metropolis." This requires one how to interpret the guide and exit signs.

5. After giving directions, have your student comment on the action planned in response to guide signs. This assures the Coach that correct responses are to be taken at the proper place. Too much deceleration before reaching the speed change lane is a common error to guard against. More collisions do occur during exiting than during merging.

6. Once on the freeway, and traffic is sufficient, additional practice can be gained with following and being followed situations. It could be a good time to practice rapid acceleration and downshifting.

LESSON 12
PASSING ONGOING VEHICLES

Passing on two-lane roads is usually a critical exercise for the application of the space and timing guidelines. Impatience and an error in timing can result in collisions with the most serious consequences. In this lesson, the steps for passing are for the acceleration pass on a two-lane road. To pass on highways with two or more lanes going the same direction, you should follow the steps for changing lanes.

TYPES OF PASSING SITUATIONS

Timed Pass

This is a situation in which you come upon an ongoing car that is traveling at a slightly slower speed than your car. You can pass the car without speeding up if you can time the pass to avoid any oncoming vehicles. You should have good sight distance for such a pass.

Flying Pass

This is a situation in which you come upon an ongoing but slow moving vehicle. You change lanes and pass at a much greater rate of speed. This can be dangerous since slow moving vehicles can steer much quicker and sharper than ones going at high speed. Therefore, you need to make sure the ongoing vehicle has not slowed down for an object or another slow moving vehicle ahead that is preparing for a left turn or lane change. A clue to this possibility would be a driveway or side road on the left side of the highway.

Acceleration Pass

This is a situation in which you are following an ongoing car that is traveling about the same speed as your car. To pass, you must speed up about 10-15 miles per hour more to overtake the car ahead. This may be the more common type of passing situation. At first, you will find it difficult to judge how much distance you will need to overtake the other car. Part of this may be due to not knowing your car's acceleration capability.

HOW TO PASS ONGOING CARS

Apply the Traffic Laws

Remember, you are not allowed to pass on a two-lane road when cars are approaching too close, and when a solid yellow line is on your side of the center line. It is illegal to pass when coming near to a hillcrest, intersection, or curve. Also, you may not pass on a bridge, in a tunnel, or near a railroad crossing.

Prepare to Pass

Start well back. Start from the "two-second" following distance. This will give you better visibility, space to speed up, and room to cut back in behind the vehicle ahead.

Signal your intentions. Give a left turn signal for a lane change, and tap the horn.

Check the mirrors. Check both mirrors and check the blindspot to your left. Then, "drift out" to the center line where you can see better.

Check ahead for safe distance. Check for a passing distance of 10 to 12 seconds visual lead. You will need at least a 9-10 second space ahead to complete the pass.

Change lanes. Pick up speed and change lanes.

Overtake the Ongoing Vehicle

Continue checks ahead. Check for roadside hazards, areas of less space, and areas of less visibility. Is there a side road on either side? Choose an escape path and be ready to drop back and try again.

Pick up speed. If the situation is "go", speed up to a 10-15 mph faster rate than the other vehicle. Down-shifting or the use of the passing gear can increase the speed up capability of your car. Check the owner's manual for the proper steps to follow.

Concentrate on path ahead. Use fringe vision for a check on the vehicle being passed and the condition of the shoulders. But, your main attention should be on the path your car is to follow.

Check for following cars. Check the mirrors again. Sometimes other drivers may try to pass you on your right side before you return to the right lane.

Return to the Right Lane

Check for front end in mirror. Look for the front end of the vehicle being passed to show up in your mirror. When this happens, you are clear of the other vehicle and ready for a return to the right lane.

Signal right. Give a right turn signal for lane change.

Change lanes to right. Be sure to maintain your speed as you steer into the right lane. Beginning drivers have a tendency to slow down at this point. They are apt to look back at the vehicle being passed to make sure of the space. This is a dangerous action and should be avoided. Concentrate on path ahead.

Cancel signal and adjust speed.

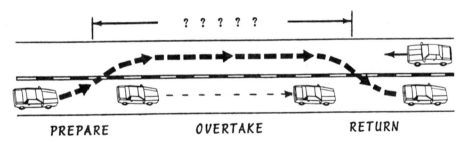

PREPARE   OVERTAKE   RETURN

ON BEING PASSED

Keep Right

As soon as you are aware that a following vehicle is about to pass, move over to the right side of your lane. This provides a better margin of space and gives the passing vehicle a better view of the road ahead.

Maintain Speed

Speeding up while being passed is against the law. Slowing down could be dangerous, too. What if the passing vehicle misjudges and wants to drop back behind you? So, always maintain speed at first.

Be Ready to Help

Once in a while a passing driver will get into a tight spot. The distance from an oncoming vehicle has been misjudged. Or, another car pulls into the passing lane from a side road. When you see there is a good chance for a head-on collision, be ready to help out. After all, your car would probably be involved in a collision so close by.

The first thing to do is to make sure what the passing driver is going to do. You can usually tell by the location of the other vehicle's front end, and perhaps, the expression on the face of the driver. If the other driver starts to slow down to cut back behind your car, then speed up to provide more space. If the other driver moves up to cut in front of you, then slow down and steer right. Take to the shoulder if necessary.

The general rule is to let the passing driver make the first move. That is the key to your actions. If each of the three drivers involved helps a little, then a collision can be prevented.

ACTIVITIES AND COACHING TIPS

1. As a passenger, the student can practice estimating how far away an oncoming car should be for the "start to pass" step. Pick a time when it may be safe to pass. Then, count how many seconds the oncoming car was from the time picked.

2. Have student practice the passing maneuver on a four lane highway. Wait behind an ongoing car until a car approaches in an opposite lane. Pass at the last second it would be safe to pass. Decide if the pass would have been safe on a two-lane highway.

3. Have student demonstrate proper passing of an ongoing car on a two-lane highway. The Coach must be alert for the tendency of beginners to cut back too soon, or to slow down some during the "return" steps.

LESSON 13
PARALLEL PARKING

Parking parallel to a curb between vehicles requires good coordination of your eyes, hands, and feet. Think of it as making a lane change while backing. All during the maneuver, you will need to make continuous checks of traffic and all four corners of your car. Try to have the car creeping slightly when steering so that you can have feedback as to whether or not your actions are sufficient. In this lesson, you will learn the basic points of reference to use. These may vary with the size of your car.

WHERE TO PARK

Legal Restrictions

Parking is usually illegal near traffic controls, railroad tracks, intersections, fire hydrants, and safety zones. Check for no parking signs and curbs painted yellow.

Gasoline Saver

When you have a full tank of gasoline, choose a place on a downgrade and in a shady area when practical. This prevents gasoline spilling over as it expands. Also, the cooler the car, the less air conditioning is required.

Space Requirements

Pick a space at least six feet greater than the length of your car. Note how close the other car is to the curb. Compare the length and width of your car with the one you pull up beside. Make adjustments if they are not the same size.

BACKING INTO A PARKING SPACE

Signal and Stop Parallel

Signal in advance and stop parallel with the vehicle you plan to park behind. Keep about three feet from this vehicle and line up the rear bumpers.

Creep Back and Steer Toward Curb

Creep backward and at the same time start steering a full turn toward the curb. When your front door is even with the rear bumper of the other car, straighten the front wheels to center steer. Then, stop and check out your position. At this point, the side of your car should make an angle of about 45 degrees with the lane lines.

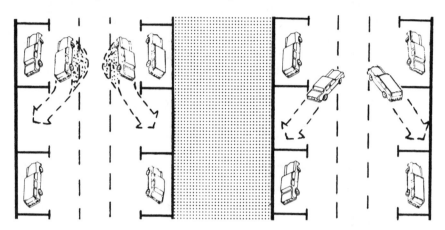

Continue backing straight along the 45 degree angle until the back end of your car is within the parking space. Stop to see if your front bumper is even with rear bumper of the car in front.

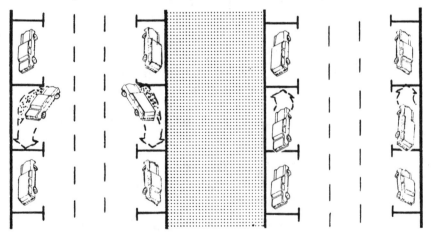

When your front bumper clears the other car, steer a full turn toward the street. Keep creeping backward until you are about parallel with the curb. When you become skilled, you will not need to make the complete stops.

Leave Car Centered in Space

As you are about parallel with the curb, straighten your wheels to center steer and stop. Then move forward and backward until your car is within twelve inches of the curb and centered in the space. If you end up on the curb or are too far from the curb, pull out on the 45 degree angle and correct the error.

PULLING OUT OF A PARKING SPACE

Back Up and Steer Toward Street

Back up while steering sharply toward the curb. This swings the front end of your car into the traffic lane. Just before reaching the car behind, steer sharply toward the street and stop. Now you have your front end and wheels pointed in the proper direction.

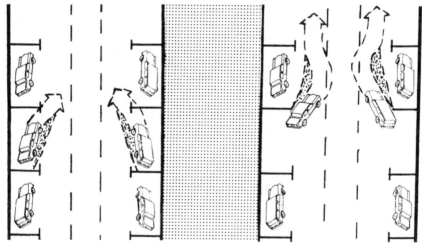

Select Gap and Move Into Street

Check traffic over your shoulder and select proper gap. Creep forward until your front end clears the rear bumper of the car ahead. Then check traffic again.

Straighten Wheels When Clear

Move forward and straighten your wheels to center steer. You should be moving out along the 45 degree angle. When your front door is even with the rear bumper of the car ahead, steer into the first traffic lane. Note that your front end will usually cross into the second traffic lane.

MAIN POINTS TO REMEMBER

- Your back bumper lines up
  with other car's back bumper.

- Your front door lines up
  with other car's back bumper.

- Your front bumper lines up
  with other car's back bumper.

ACTIVITIES AND COACHING TIPS

1. Obtain a toy wagon and set up parking stalls with cardboard boxes. Have student practice parking wagon. A riding type lawn mower may be used for practice when available.

2. On a vacant parking lot, have student practice making lane changes while backing.

3. When riding with relatives or friends, student should observe how they position their car for parking. They can be asked to explain the steps they follow.

4. Time can be saved with a model demonstration by the Coach. Student is asked to note when and how much steering is needed. The relationship between steering wheel actions and the car movement can be shown.

5. Find a residential area with level streets where there are a few cars parked along the curb. Have student pull up parallel by one car at a time and practice parking behind each one. Then, progress to business district for parking between two cars. Have student practice on both sides of a one-way street.

LESSON 14
DRIVING AT NIGHT

Your chance of having a collision is at least two times greater at night than in the daytime. If you have an eye problem, the odds are greater. Driving at night is more dangerous because of reduced visibility. Pedestrians and drivers are more apt to be under the influence of drugs and alcohol. And, the problem of fatigue is a more serious problem at night.

You can learn to be a safe driver at night just as many professional drivers have. First, you must be aware of the special problems you face. Then, you must compensate by adjusting speed and eye habits. Finally, you must learn to control fatigue and deal with the drivers who are impaired.

As you practice driving at night, pick first the streets and highways you have driven on. Note the differences between day and night. Gradually, practice driving in a variety of traffic and roadway conditions.

PREPARATION FOR DRIVING AT NIGHT

Clean Surfaces

Keep the windshield, rear window, and lights clean. A dirty or fogged over windshield can reduce your night vision and increase glare from other lights. A dirty headlight can cut in half the supply of light. Drivers who must wear glasses, should keep these lenses clean.

Locate the Light Switches

Know where and how the light switches operate. Practice using them in the daytime so you can find them quickly by sense of touch.

Check for Burned Out Bulbs

Every two to three months and before a long trip, walk around your car after the various lights have been turned on. Remember to put the selector lever in reverse so you can check out the back-up lights.

Check for Windshield Washer Fluid

When you fill up with gasoline, check the level of the windshield washer fluid. Make sure it is an anti-freeze.

Carry Emergency Equipment

You should carry flares and/or reflective devices in case of emergencies. These provide for the proper identification of a disabled vehicle. Carry a flashlight.

Check for Headlight Aim

Headlights need to be aligned or aimed properly. High beams or bright lights can lose a third of their effectiveness if they are out of line. Improperly aimed low beams or dimmers can cause glare problems for drivers of oncoming vehicles.

High

Beams

High beams should light up the highway from side to side for about 300 feet. Low beams light up only your side of the highway for about 250 feet. If oncoming drivers flash their lights at you when you are driving with the low beams on, they are suggesting your lights may be out of adjustment.

To check the alignment of headlights, stop your car about twenty feet from a garage door. Turn on the high beams and then the low beams. The high beams should light up the whole door. The low beams should light up an area slightly down and to the right. Screws on either side of the headlights are turned for making adjustments.

WISE USE OF LIGHTS

Headlights

The headlights are turned on by a switch located on dash or the lever on the left side of the steering column. The parking lights, tail lights, side markers, and the dash lights come on along with the headlights.

Headlights are to be turned on from sunset to sunrise. Also, they need to be used when visibility is poor during the day. If in doubt, turn them on. In many situations, your headlights may not help you see better, but they really will help others see you.

When the high beams are turned on, a blue light on the instrument panel comes on. Use these bright lights only when you can't see well enough to drive with the low beams or dimmers. Glare from the high beams tend to blind the driver of an oncoming car. So, you must always dim your lights at least 500 feet from oncoming vehicles. Also, you must dim your lights when following within 300 feet of another vehicle. Increase your following distance to three seconds at night.

Low

Beams

If the driver of an oncoming vehicle has the bright lights on, flash your lights from low beam to high beam and back to low beam. Don't over react or get angry. Concentrate on keeping to right side and getting by. Two blinded drivers create a worse situation than having only one driver blinded for a short time.

Parking Lights

Parking lights may be turned on separately from the headlights. They show your car is parked or standing. Do not drive your car with just the parking lights on.

Hazard Lights

A hazard warning switch flashes on and off all four signal lights. They warn other drivers that you are stopped because of a problem or emergency. They are not intended for use when your car is in motion. For an exception, some truck drivers may use these flashers to indicate their truck is a slow-moving vehicle going uphill.

Interior Lights

The dome light comes on when doors are opened and

goes off when doors are closed. The dome light may be turned on or off by rotating the light switch. When parked along the shoulder of a highway, you may turn on the dome light to help show you are not moving.

The brightness of the instrument panel light can be adjusted by rotating the light switch after it is turned on. It is best for these panel lights to be dimmed while driving. A separate switch turns on a small beam of light for reading maps or other material.

EYE HABITS FOR DRIVING AT NIGHT

Obviously, no one can see as well at night as during the day. How well you do see at night will depend on your ability to see under low illumination, the ability to see against glare, and the ability to recover from glare and brightness. These abilities vary from person to person. They decrease with age for everyone.

Some driver's eyes may not adapt well to low illumination. Such persons should avoid driving at night or at least limit their driving to well lighted areas.

Adapting from Light to Dark

Everyone has experienced what it is like to walk out of a brightly lighted building into darkness. Your eyes take time to adjust to such a contrast. So, when you walk out of a brightly lighted room at night and get into your car, wait at least five minutes before driving. Also, it is best to drive slowly for a few minutes.

When you have been outside in the bright sunshine for the afternoon, your eyes will take at least thirty minutes or more to adapt after the sun goes down. If you wear dark sun glasses when you are in the sun, you will not need so long for the eyes to adapt. Of course, you must take off your sunglasses before driving at night.

Glare Recovery

As you drive at night, the headlights of oncoming cars will actually light up more of the highway. This can be helpful, but the glare from these same headlights can also blind you for two or three seconds. Therefore, you must modify your scanning habits for such situations.

As you approach other vehicles at night, do not

continue to scan from one side of the roadway to the other. Instead, use the right edge of the roadway or lane as your main point of reference. Then scan quickly

to the center of your path and back to the edge. Scan also from the far edge of the area lighted ahead to the near front and repeat. It is most important that you not stare or fix your eyes on any area for more than two seconds. By using such scanning methods until the oncoming vehicles go by, you can control headlight glare. At the same time, you can see the surface conditions, pedestrians, and the relative position of the oncoming vehicles. You still must be able to tell if any vehicles are drifting toward the center line.

You can receive glare from your rear view mirrors. In such a case, adjust the mirrors. If you do become temporarily blinded, slow down and keep well to the right until your eyes readjust.

It is best not to smoke while driving at night. The nicotine and carbon monoxide can reduce your vision. And, the smoke makes a dark film on the windshield.

SPEED ADJUSTMENTS FOR NIGHT DRIVING

Reduce Speed

At night, you are always driving under conditions of reduced visibility. So, reduce your speed at least ten miles per hour from the daytime speed on rural highways. This would not apply to well lighted urban streets.

Do Not Overdrive Your Headlights

This rule is just common sense. Your seeing distance ahead should never be less than your braking distance of four seconds. For example, assume you will need 300 feet to stop when traveling sixty miles per hour. If you can only see 250 feet ahead with your headlights, then you would be overdriving your headlights.

CONTROL OF FATIGUE

There are two types of fatigue that can affect your driving. One is due to a lack of rest and sleep. The other is known as operational fatigue. Operational fatigue results mostly from continued hours of driving without stopping. Fighting heavy traffic and bad road conditions will wear a person down. At night, eyestrain is another factor to take into account.

Fatigue is a serious problem and is the cause of many collisions. It affects all the physical and mental abilities used in driving. A tired driver usually becomes irritable and over-reacts to problems. Too often, drivers fight to stay awake. Then they resort to "stay awake" pills which can make matters worse.

Take a Break

When you must drive some distance at night, plan to make regular rest stops every hour. Always get some exercise each time you stop. Avoid eating heavy foods. If you go into a restaurant for refreshments, wear sunglasses to offset the bright lights.

On a long trip, a good time to stop for rest would be your regular bed time. Your body is used to rest and sleep at a certain time. At this time you will get tired quicker. If you get drowsy, take a short nap. Wash your face with cold water.

Vary Your Activities

It is wise to change speeds slightly from time to time. Open a vent or window for some fresh air. Talk about the trip plan and road conditions. Take turns driving. If you are alone, sing occasionally. Change your seat position and seat adjustment.

Avoid Taking Pep Pills

If you force a tired body to stay awake with drugs, serious problems can result. When the effect of these drugs wear off, a driver goes to sleep without warning. Alcohol is a depressant that drivers should never use.

SUMMARY

- Keep windshield, rear window, and headlights clean. Check headlights for proper alignment.

- Turn on headlights at sunset. Dim them when facing or following other vehicles.

- When parking along a roadway, use the hazard and dome lights. Carry a flashlight.

- Use sunglasses in bright sunshine before driving at night. Give eyes time to adapt to darkness.

- After coming out of a brightly lighted building, wait five minutes before driving.

- Look to the far edges of the headlight beams. Do not focus on the middle of the beams.

- When facing other headlights, focus eyes on the right side of lane or roadway. Scan from right edge to center of path and back.

- Never overdrive your headlights. Increase the following and stopping distances at night.

- Plan regular rest stops. When driving past your regular bedtime, expect drowsiness.

ACTIVITIES AND COACHING TIPS

1. Students can use a stop watch to find out how long it takes a person's eyes to adapt to darkness after coming out of a brightly lighted building.

2. The student should practice first on the highways and streets he or she has driven on during the day. Use commentary driving to note the differences.

3. Student should practice switching the headlights back and forth between low and high beam. Have student measure in seconds the farthest distance he or she can see ahead with both the high and low beam lights.

4. When facing other cars at night, have student practice proper scanning without becoming temporarily blinded. Can the student tell how far the side of the oncoming vehicle is from the center line.

LESSON 15
DRIVING A CAR WITH A CLUTCH

To drive a manual transmission car, you must be able to select and change gears by hand. This will require learning how to coordinate the use of a clutch with the gearshift lever and the gas pedal. Operating the gearshift lever is similar to using the selector lever, and you will find it easy to use. Learning how to use the clutch skillfully to start and stop a manual transmission car is the difficult part. That is the purpose of this lesson.

HOW THE CLUTCH WORKS

Purpose of a Clutch

The clutch consists of two rotating discs which can be moved apart or together by a clutch pedal. When they are together, they connect the motor with the transmission (gearbox) and drive wheels. When the discs are moved apart by the clutch pedal, the motor and gearbox are disconnected. This allows the gears to be changed by hand with the gearshift lever. The clutch also allows the motor to be started and run without moving the car.

Clutch Pedal Down

The clutch pedal is always located left of the brake pedal. When it is pushed down all the way to the floor of the car, the two clutch discs are moved apart.

Clutch Pedal Up

When the clutch pedal is all the way up from the floor, the two clutch discs are forced together. They then are held together firmly as they rotate around.

Contact Point

The contact point is where the clutch pedal is held part way up from the floor and the rotating discs start touching or rubbing each other. Your foot can feel this contact taking place, and it is then that the car begins to move. This point is called the friction point also.

Riding the Clutch

When you allow your left foot to rest lightly on the clutch pedal while your car is moving, you are "riding" the clutch. Such a habit can increase wear on the clutch and waste gasoline.

GEARSHIFT LEVER POSITIONS

Number and Location

The standard transmission has at least three speeds forward and one for backing. These positions along with neutral form an "H" pattern. Many gearshift cars have four or five speeds forward. The gearshift lever or stick-shift is usually located on the floor.

Neutral Position

You can tell where neutral is because it is the only position that allows the lever to be moved sideways. The car is out of gear when in neutral. Therefore, it allows the motor to run when the car is stopped. Neutral should be used for starting the car. Don't park and leave the car in neutral.

Reverse Gear

Reverse (R) has maximum power and should be used for backing the car at speeds less than 15 mph. Be sure the car is stopped before shifting to "R".

First Gear or Low

Always use first gear for moving the car from a stop-ped position and for speeds up to 10-15 mph. It is to be used for heavy pulling up steep hills, in mud or sand, and in deep snow. Most owner's manuals suggest a top speed of 35 miles per hour.

Second Gear

Second has moderate power, and is used mainly for increasing the speed (15-25 mph) and momentum of the car for higher gears. It is a good gear for driving in heavy stop and go traffic.

Third Gear or High

Third gear is used for normal driving or speeds of 25 miles per hour and up.

Fourth Gear

Fourth is a low-powered gear for speeds above 35 mph and for saving gasoline. It may be called overdrive.

STARTING WITH A CLUTCH

Starting the Motor

- Check the park brake.
- Push the clutch down.
- Put gearshift lever in neutral (N).
- Set choke if necessary.
- Turn key to start and release.
- Read gauges while motor idles.

```
1      3      5
|      |      |
|----[ N ]----|
|      |      |
2      4      R
```

Except when your car stalls in traffic, always start the motor with the clutch down and the park brake on. The brake prevents the car from rolling. The clutch is held down in case the gearshift is not in "N" or you want to shift quickly. Some cars won't start unless the clutch is down all the way.

Moving Out in First and "R"

- Hold clutch pedal down.
- Shift to first or reverse.
- Move clutch to contact point.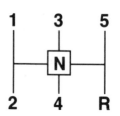
- Press slightly on gas pedal and release park brake.
- Let clutch all the way up.

As you let the clutch pedal up slowly to the contact point and hold for a second, note the change in the sound of the motor. Your foot should also sense the clutch disc rubbing together. Then press the gas pedal for a steady fast idle and release the park brake. The amount of gas needed depends on whether your car is on a roadway that is level, uphill, or downhill.

Once the car starts to move, you should slowly let the clutch up the rest of the way. If you let the clutch up too soon or too quickly, the car starts jerking or stalls out. Remember, the action of the left and right feet must be well coordinated. When the left foot is coming up, the right foot is going down some.

Clutch Control for Creeping

- Have gearshift in first or "R" (clutch down).
- Move clutch pedal to contact point and hold.
- Press and hold gas pedal for steady fast idle
- Ease clutch pedal up or down just a little.

With an automatic transmission, you use the gas pedal for creeping. With a manual transmission, the creeping action is controlled by the clutch. You get the creeping by holding the gas pedal steady while making very small movements of the clutch pedal at the contact point. When the clutch pedal is eased up some from the contact point, the car will creep faster. The closer the clutch comes to the contact point, the slower the car creeps.

It will take patience and much practice for your feet to coordinate these and other such actions. But, they will soon sense what to do automatically. Then you will have mastered the clutch.

Starting Uphill in Traffic

- Hold right foot on brake after stop (clutch down).
- Shift to first gear or low.
- Move clutch up to contact point and hold.
- Move right foot to gas pedal quickly for fast idle.
- Let clutch up slowly all the way.
- Press on gas pedal as needed.

Learn to move your right foot from the brake to the gas pedal just as your left foot moves toward the contact point. The trick is to keep your left foot from going too far past the contact point before the gas pedal is pushed down enough and held steady.

Your timing must be just right or the car will begin to roll backward. Then, you will tend to overcompensate and let the clutch up too much which results in the car jerking badly or the motor stalling. If the car starts rolling back too much, put the clutch down and brake to a stop. Then, start over until you get in control. If you are holding up traffic and get nervous, use the hand brake method.

STOPPING AND SECURING

Stopping in First or "R"

- Check traffic and signal.
- Push clutch down and hold.
- Let up on gas pedal.
- Push brake for smooth stop.
- Shift to neutral.

In first or reverse, the car has maximum power and is to be driven at slow speeds. Therefore, you should push the clutch down first before using the brake pedal. Otherwise, you get a jerky stop. These same stops apply for second gear.

Stopping in Third or Fourth

- Check traffic and signal.
- Let up on gas pedal.
- Apply brake lightly.
- Push clutch down and hold.
- Continue braking to a stop.

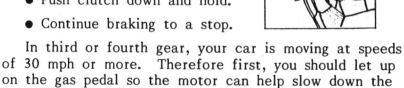

In third or fourth gear, your car is moving at speeds of 30 mph or more. Therefore first, you should let up on the gas pedal so the motor can help slow down the car. This saves gasoline and wear on the brakes. Then, use the brake to slow down to about 10 mph before pushing the clutch down.

Secure Car for Parking

- Hold clutch down all the way.
- Shut off all accessories.
- Shut off engine.
- Shift to "R" or first.
- Put park brake on.

When parking and leaving the gearshift car, you should always leave the car in gear for extra safety.

SHIFTING TO HIGHER GEARS

Shifting from First to Second

- Speed up in first to 10-15 mph.
- Push clutch down and let up on gas.
- Shift the lever from first to second.
- Move clutch up to contact point and hesitate.
- Push on gas pedal some.
- Let clutch up and speed up.

Speed in first gear may vary with the conditions. On a downgrade, your car will pick up speed as the clutch goes down. On an uphill road, you may need to be going faster since the car will slow down as soon as the clutch goes down.

Shifting from Second to Third

- Speed up in second to 15-20 mph.
- Push clutch pedal down.
- Let up on gas and move clutch to contact point.
- Press on gas pedal and let up on clutch.

You will not need to hesitate so long at the contact point since the car has picked up momentum. Check your owner's manual for the suggested speed range to do shifting to higher gears. Note that whenever the left foot goes down on the clutch, the right foot lets up on the gas pedal. Then, when the left foot comes up, the right foot starts moving down. Remember the motor sounds for each position.

HOW TO DOWNSHIFT

You have learned how to shift up from one gear to another. Now, you need to learn how to shift down from a higher gear to a lower one while the car is in motion. How often and when you will need to downshift depends on the size of your car's motor, the number of gear postions, and the roadway conditions.

Downshifting from Third to Second

- Let up on gas pedal.
- Push clutch pedal down.
- Shift from 3rd to 2nd.
- Press gas pedal gently.
- Let clutch pedal up slowly.
- Adjust speed for conditions.

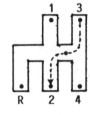

After shifting to second, you should increase the speed slightly just before letting up on the clutch. You are trying to match the motor speed with the speed of the car. This allows the gears to mesh easier and smoother. When letting up the clutch, ease through the point of contact. After the clutch is up, the amount of pressure on the gas pedal depends on whether you were downshifting for slowing down or for picking up speed. Use the same steps for downshifting from higher gears.

Downshifting from Second to First

- Let up on the gas pedal.
- Push clutch pedal down.
- Brake almost to a stop.
- Shift from second to first.
- Move clutch to contact point, and
- Press on gas pedal at same time.
- Ease up on clutch, and adjust speed.

When you are going up a steep hill, you should try to carry out the steps quickly. Otherwise, your car could start rolling backward. In such a case, stop and start over or use the park brake method for starting up.

WHEN TO DOWNSHIFT

Downshifting for Turns

When turning at intersections, you will usually have to slow down and shift down. Mostly, this should be second. As a rule, shift down before making the turn. You will have better traction and steering control. If you should misjudge, downshift just as you come out of the turn. Do not coast around the corner with the clutch down.

If you must go up a steep hill after making a sharp turn, it is best to downshift to first before turning. This is better than getting part way around the corner, and then finding out you don't have enough power in second.

Downshifting for Traffic Conditions

Traffic Conflicts -- Once you identify a conflict up ahead, be ready to downshift. You may need to slow down or pick up speed.

Passing and Merging -- These situations may require a quick pick up in speed. Second gear may be best.

Slow-moving or Heavy Traffic -- If you have a four or five speed transmission, it may be best to use only the first three gear positions for most city traffic.

Downshifting for Roadway Conditions

Less Traction -- If you identify slippery spots ahead that require a slower speed, be sure to downshift well ahead of the area. Otherwise, the downshifting could cause a side skid. When the clutch is let up too quickly, the drive wheels may spin and cause loss of control. When driving on very slippery pavement for any distance, second gear may be best. But, you must use the gas pedal very gently.

Steep Uphill -- As you start up a steep hill, listen for motor sounds to note if there is any pick up left. If the engine starts laboring in fourth or third, it is time to shift down.

Steep Downhill -- On a long steep downhill, shifting to a lower gear allows the motor drag to help keep the car from picking up too much momentum. Hard use of the brakes for a period of time can cause them to overheat and be less effective.

If you will want to shift to first gear, it is best to shift down at the top of the hill. If you must shift part way down the hill, slow the car with the brakes and shift to second. If you will need first gear, you should brake almost to a stop before trying to shift down.

Other Roadway Conditions -- Railroad crossings and changes in space or visibility may call for downshifting.

GENERAL GUIDELINES TO REMEMBER

- Move left hand to top of steering wheel when you are shifting.

- Remember the motor sounds for each position.

- Rehearse in your mind the shifting patterns.

- Do not coast around corners with clutch down.

- Anticipate the gear needed for each situation.

- When shifting, match motor speed with car speed.

- Skipping gears when downshifting is OK, but it is not for shifting up.

- Always shift to first after stopping.

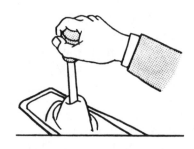

ACTIVITIES AND COACHING TIPS

1. As with any car used, the owner's manual should be reviewed for any specific procedures and shifting speed ranges that are recommended for that model.

2. An off-street area should be selected first for those who have not driven an automatic transmission car. For others, most of this lesson can be conducted on a level street or rural blacktop with little other traffic. A roadway with a long and gradual upgrade will be needed for one part. Then, practice can take place in a variety of roadway conditions and traffic situations.

3. Learning how to coordinate the actions and timing between the clutch pedal, the gearshift lever, and the gas pedal will take much patience and repitition. Therefore, a series of step-by-step practice exercises or drills must be set up and conducted.

4. Before any drills or exercises are started, the coach should give a model demonstration of starting, stopping, shifting to all gears, and downshifting.

5. On a level side street or parking lot, have the student start the engine, practice shifting to all gear positions with the clutch down, and shut off the engine. This is repeated until the student can use the gearshift without looking at it. Next, have student move car forward in low a few feet and stop. Then, have the car moved backward a few feet. Repeat this forward and backward drill until student easily senses the location of the clutch contact or friction point. Include clutch control for creeping.

6. On a straight and level stretch of roadway, have the student practice shifting from first gear to all other forward gears. Also, guide the practice for stopping from each forward gear position.

7. On a roadway with a slight upgrade, have student practice starting and stopping in first gear without using the park brake. Then, practice parking along a curb both uphill and downhill.

8. On a straight stretch of roadway, have the student practice downshifting. After some proficiency is demonstrated, provide plenty of opportunities for the practice of downshifting in each of the situations described in the lesson.

9. On a rural highway, have student practice turning off of and onto the highway. Also, guide the practice of entering and exiting at interchanges.

HOW TO SAVE GASOLINE AND MONEY

By using the following safe and efficient practices, you can get at least thirty percent more miles per gallon of gasoline. You not only save gasoline and money, but you can cut down on air pollution as well.

Plan Trips Wisely

- Telephone first to avoid wasted trips.
- Combine several errands into one trip.
- Run errands when traffic is lightest.
- Pick a route with the fewest stops and starts and avoids back tracking.
- Use air conditioner wisely and park in shade.
- On long trips, plan for rest stops. Keep windows closed at highway speeds.

Starting and Stopping

- Avoid pumping the gas pedal when starting motor.
- After thirty seconds, drive to warm up. The engine will warm up faster if car is in motion.
- Speed up smoothly but quickly. Low gears consume more gasoline.
- Let engine slow car before braking to stop.
- At drive-in places, turn off engine rather than let it idle. It saves gasoline and cuts down on pollution.
- Don't rev up engine before shutting it off.

Adjust Speed and Position for Conditions

- Use light gas pedal pressure.
- Blend with the flow of traffic.
- Drive at common and steady speeds.
- Adjust speed for timing of signal lights.
- Anticipate traffic changes ahead.
- Maintain proper space margins.
- Make changes in position smoothly. Avoid weaving.
- Slow down when driving in high winds.
- Slow down going into curves. Speed up coming out of curves.
- Use momentum for going uphill. Use gravity for going downhill.

Practice Preventive Maintenance

- Keep tires properly inflated.
- Keep front wheels properly aligned.
- Get a tune-up when recommended.
- Change oil and filter as recommended.
- Use gasoline of proper octane rating.
- Don't top off when filling the gasoline tank.
- Keep a record of regular maintenance, and make a check of miles per gallon at least monthly.
- After five days of city driving, go out on a high speed highway to burn up unwanted deposits.

Drive Clean - Drive Light - Drive Right

PARENT-TEEN DRIVER CONTRACT

In most states, parents have some legal responsibility for the safe driving performance of their teenagers. The privilege for an unmarried minor to drive is given only with the consent of the parents or a guardian. If this privilege is abused in the judgment of the consenting adult, then the driving privilege can be cancelled when a written request is sent to the proper state licensing official.

Studies have shown that school grades really suffer when students are permitted unrestricted use of either a family car or a personal car. There is also a greater chance that traffic law violations and collisions will occur. Therefore, it is wise for parents to keep control of the car keys until a teenager has graduated from high school. Most teenagers will appreciate this parental guidance and help.

When the family car is shared, a greater atmosphere of mutual trust and understanding can exist. Then, problems that arise can be discussed more openly. Even though many teenagers do not use drugs, they will still be under much pressure at parties and in cars where the abuse of alcohol and other drugs take place. Parents can have a more positive influence than many realize.

Before a young person is allowed to use a family car, certain conditions need to be discussed and agreed upon. Will the maintenance and fuel costs be shared? Who will pay for traffic violations? Will the use of the car be linked to school grades? These and any regulations such as the use of seat belts, should be identified in a clear and concise way.

Once the conditions are agreed to, they need to be put in writing. Such an agreement is then signed by both parents and their teenager. When this formal agreement is promptly and fairly enforced, it can help lead to responsible behavior, economical operation, and a safer performance.

A free copy of a parent-teen driver contract is available from Safety Enterprises, 1010 South Summit, Bloomington, Illinois 61701.